Resources for Teaching Gerontology

Resources for Teaching Gerontology

Verle Waters, Editor

National League for Nursing Press • New York
Pub. No.14-2608

Verle Waters, MA, RN,
is Dean Emerita, Ohlone College, Fremont, California, and Project
Consultant, Community College-Nursing Home Partnership.

Contents

FOREWORD

The need for educating professional nurses in the care of older adults is of critical importance today and will continue well into the 21st century. As the population of the United States and the world continues to increase in age, the unique health care needs of older adults will be ever more prevalent in all home-based settings, community health programs, long-term care, and acute care facilities. These health care needs are based on the developmental tasks needing to be accomplished by aging persons which affords them the opportunity to be productive citizens. For these reasons the book, *Resources for Teaching Gerontology*, edited by my good friend and professional colleague, Verle Waters, MA, RN, serves such a useful purpose at this moment in time.

The explanations provided in this text regarding what constitutes aging and the distinctive holistic health care needs of this population aid the reader in understanding that the older person is not to be placed in a category of "aging." Rather, each older adult is to be viewed as a special and rare individual with a history peculiar to that person. The cultural, social, psychological, physiological, and spiritual dimensions of each older person are an unusual blueprint of a personality not ever to be captured again in just that special way. It is this instruction that is so important for every professional nurse who is privileged to assist older adults in the provision of nursing care that makes gerontological nursing so rewarding. Each older adult is to be seen as one person, not the stereotypic image society has portrayed in cartoons, movies, and the TV commercials.

As an Advisory Board Member to the Community College–Nursing Home Partnership Project, it was my privilege to observe the deepening of understanding of gerontological nursing by the project directors who committed themselves to incorporating into the Associate Degree Nursing Programs curriculum content about the older adult and clinical experiences that supported that content. The sophistication with which they developed teaching materials so that nursing students might grasp a positive approach to older adults gave my great pleasure. It is through these course descriptions, clinical practice opportunities, and classroom exercises as identified in this text that nurses will gain the necessary insights into the appropriate quality care for older adult.

I congratulate my colleague on an excellent text and a most welcome addition to the gerontologic literature. Here is a text that should be found in every nurse's library so that nurses who care for the older adult of the future are armed with appropriate knowledge, skill, competencies, and positive attitudes as this segment of the population increases.

Sister Rose Therese Bahr
ASC, PhD, RN, FAAN

ACKNOWLEDGEMENTS

The Community College-Nursing Home Partnership Project was in existence for seven years. Over that long and busy period of time, many people contributed to its success; it would not have been the same, or as good, without their support, enthusiasm, and hard work. There is not space or time to thank each of them individually, or to acknowledge the unique contribution of each. This note of appreciation to all of the fine people who became part of the project in many ways for many time periods will have to do.

Helen Grace, PhD, RN, now Vice President at the W.K. Kellogg Foundation, began as our project manager, and made us feel secure and special because she continued in that role long after her assignment at the Foundation was expanded and elevated. Her belief in this project has been felt by every staff member at each project site, and it strengthened us.

Susan Sherman, MA, RN, Head, Department of Nursing, Community College of Philadelphia, has been Project Administrator since 1990, providing leadership and direction during these years of disseminating project findings, and bringing to closure what had become a far-flung operation. We relied upon her insights and instincts, along with her considerable organizational and administrative skills.

The authors of these pages, other than the editor, were project coordinators at each of the six demonstration sites. The coordinators, listed below, were the front-line workers on this project, in every sense of the term. Each of them was a leader in her own project area; as members of a close-knit group, they sustained and enriched each other and our project.

Elaine Tagliareni, MS, RNC, Community College of Philadelphia

Gail Cobe, MSN, RN, Ohlone College

Patricia Bentz, MSN, RNC and *Janice E. Ellis,* PhD, RN, Shoreline College

Mary Ellen Simmons, MS, RNC, Triton College

Ann Carignan, MSN, RNC, Valencia Community College

Mary Ann Anderson, MS, RN, CNA, Weber State University

The support and active participation of the nursing program dean or director at each of the six campus sites that conducted the demonstration phase of the project 1986-1990 and the dissemination phase 1990-1993 was an essential ingredient in project success. They were:

Gerry L. Hansen, EdD, RN, Weber State University
Ann Miller, MA, RNC, Valencia Community College
Carol Casten, MSN, RN, (Deceased), Trition College 1987-1992
Connie Allekian, MSN, RN, Triton College, 1992-1993
Celia L. Hartley, MN, RN, Shoreline Community College (now at College of the Desert, CA)
Sharlene Limon, MS, RN, Ohlone College
Susan Sherman, MA, RN, Community College of Philadelphia

The so-called second generation schools, community college nursing programs that became part of the project during the 1990-1993 dissemination phase, represent nearly a third of the associate degree programs in the nation. We could not overstate our pride and pleasure in their participation, in the eagerness with which many of the faculty embraced project purposes and activities. Many of them devised new learning activities or adapted old ones to teaching about gerontology included in these pages.

The project has benefited immensely from the assistance of an active advisory committee. We are indebted to the following members who became a part of the endeavor, offering criticism, suggestions, and encouragement, and opening doors that expanded our influence:

Sister Rose Therese Bahr, PhD, RN, FAAN
1400 S. Sheridan
Wichita, KS 67201

Richard W. Besdine, MD
Director
Travelers Center on Aging
University of Connecticut Health Center
Farmington, CT 06032-9989

Judith Braun, PhD, RN
Executive Director
The Washington House
5100 Fillmore Ave.
Alexandria, VA 22311

James T. McCall, FACHCA
Consultant
4174 Sunbury Rd.
Galena, OH 43021

Mathey Mazey, EdD, RN, FAAN
Division of Nursing
New York University
429 Shimkin Hall
Washington Square
New York, NY 10003

Robert E. Parilla, PhD
President
Montgomery College
900 Hungerford Drive
Rockville, MD 20850

Donna A. Peters, PhD, RN, FAAN
Former Director, CHAP
National League for Nursing
350 Hudson St.
New York, NY 10014

Vera Reublinger, MA, RNC
Consultant
1843 Mintwood Place NW #206
Washington, DC 20009

Leopold G. Selker, PhD
Dean
College of Associated Health Professions
University of Illinois
P.O. Box 6998
Chicago, IL 60612

Joan Warden, RN, CDONA/LTC
President
NADONA/LTC
10999 Reed Hartman Hwy., Suite 234
Cincinnati, OH 45242

Chapter 1

Introduction

This book is dedicated to teachers of nursing and to the future patients their students will care for, most of whom will be 65 years of age and older. Nursing educators have increasingly become aware of the facts about the aging patient population (in the year 2000 it is expected that nearly half of all RNs will be in elder care.[1]), and it is fast becoming general faculty knowledge that gerontology in the nursing curriculum is a necessity.

Such a change in the nursing curriculum was undertaken in 1986 in a W.K. Kellogg-funded project, entitled *The Community College-Nursing Home Partnership*, which engaged faculty in six project sites in the demonstration of new gerontologic nursing learning experiences for basic students. The nursing faculty in the six project schools prepared a teaching handbook entitled *Teaching Gerontology: The Curriculum Imperative*[2], which contained guidelines for adding or increasing gerontologic nursing instruction, and strategies for clinical education in the nursing home. *Teaching Gerontology* has enjoyed an enthusiastic and responsive readership. Those of us who were involved in the projects and who were the contributing writers and editors of the handbook have since received a number of requests for more examples of teaching/learning activities than were included in the appendix of *Teaching Gerontology*. We have written and edited this resource manual in response to those requests.

The teaching/learning activities in this manual were created by nursing teachers in some 20 nursing programs across the country. In the years since the 1991 publication of *Teaching Gerontology*, each of the six demonstration site programs has recruited within its geographic region a second generation of project affiliates. Variously called "cluster schools," "ambassadors," "leaders," "protege schools," or "member schools," second generation nursing programs were those within a region interested in adding gerontologic content and a clinical rotation in the nursing home. In a real sense, the last three years of the project stirred a ripple of activities which resulted in an impressively large network of nurse faculty throughout the country working to improve the preparation of basic students for future roles in the care of elderly patients. Faculty in second generation project schools not only adopted learning activities developed in demonstration sites, but also created and adapted new approaches to the teaching of gerontological nursing. Many of them are included here.

In the 1991 publication, it was noted that there was no clear definition of or agreement about the core of gerontologic nursing knowledge and skills required for registered nursing practice.

> *Gerontological nursing content in the nursing curriculum is vaguely defined. A teacher or faculty committee beginning the task of identifying what to teach finds few guidelines for selecting the knowledge and skills necessary for nursing practice. Concepts that make up the body of knowledge about aging needed for nursing practice derive from a number of disciplines: biology, psychology, sociology, medical sciences, and pathology. An expanding body of nursing literature provides some assistance to educators in determining what is most important to teach. But the decisions about what to select and what to emphasize—about balancing the time spent on normal aging and the well elder's health needs with time spent on the commonly occurring late life illness and nursing needs of patients, or about allocating clinical time to long-term care settings as well as acute care—are difficult.[3]*

The search continues for a definition of the "right" gerontologic nursing content and the "best" clinical experience. Faculty choices about the "best" or "most important" knowledge or clinical learning experiences are arguably more problematic than for most other subjects in the curriculum because attitudes toward the care of the elderly and the chronically ill are laced with stereotypical images, professional values, personal fears, and remembered negative experiences. For example, when faculty discuss new learning experiences for students in gerontologic nursing, the cloud of negative images, values, and experiences can obscure and distort the discussion. In these discussions, for instance, the nursing home may be excluded as a clinical placement. It is a given that faculty values and attitudes play an important role in the selection of learning experiences.

Even where faculty are initially reluctant to endorse clinical education in the nursing home, a learning experience with ambulatory, relatively healthy elders appears to be an acceptable first step in increasing curriculum attention to gerontologic nursing. Some experts express the opinion that student clinical experiences which begin with those well older persons who are models of coping and surviving in the face of multiple life changes will change negative student attitudes to positive attitudes.[4] We begin this manual, then, with several examples of learning activities requiring interaction with relatively healthy older people; these examples are designed to expand the student's understanding of normal aging processes, and to prompt new attitudes toward aging and toward nursing of older people.

One of the demonstration site programs, and a number of other associate degree programs, have for a long time placed beginning students in a nursing home or other long-term care setting to meet objectives related to foundational skills and basic nursing knowledge. We know of programs which have recently begun to use a long-term care clinical in the first term of study because of shrinking acute-care placements suited to beginners. There are arguments both for and against the placement of beginning students in the nursing home. Some argue that the stable and predictable environment of extended care facilities is appropriate to beginning students who are learning the nursing process and elements of basic care.[5] Others contend that an initial clinical experience with a frail, demented, or chronically ill older person may reinforce stereotypes and devalue the complexity of the clinical decision-making process.[6] If there is any rule of thumb in faculty decision making it is that faculty and clinical agency staff members' attitudes exert great influence over student attitudes and learning. Therefore, we feel it is important to proceed with plans for clinical education that can be honestly supported and promoted by those faculty and staff. We have included learning experiences for use early in the student's program of study with the hoped for result that positive feelings will develop about nursing frail, dependent elders.

From the beginning of the project we have taken the position that to effectively teach gerontologic nursing knowledge and skills and to prepare graduates for the RN role in long-term care settings, the faculty must include clinical experience devoted to that purpose late in the student's program of study. An important serendipitous finding during the years of the project is that a second-level nursing home clinical strengthens the student's education far beyond the gain in gerontological nursing competence.[7] While allocating time late in the student's program of study for clinical education in the nursing home is a major, often difficult step, in our experience the faculty who work through the challenges become convinced themselves of the unique and exceptional value of the nursing home as a learning environment. We have therefore included case studies and other clinical teaching activities and strategies that have been found effective for advanced-level students.

Any serious examination of nursing care issues related to the care of older adults will soon reveal profound ethical dilemmas. At Ohlone College and other project sites, faculty closely studied the learning activities which seemed appropriate in preparing students to face the hard ethical problems which they will meet in nursing practice. Examples of these learning activities, accompanied by an annotated bibliography, are included in this volume.

We have included, in addition to the bibliography described above, annotations for film and video resources in this field, a comprehensive annotated list of textbooks in gerontologic nursing, and a list of community-based organizations and individuals to enrich learning.

This resource book represents the experience and thought of a sizeable number of nursing teachers who have provided leadership to their own program faculty; they now share their recommendations and ideas with the wider audience represented by you, our readers. The activities described in these pages will not be perfect for your teaching needs; we think they will stimulate you to create new and better learning events for your students.

[1] Wells, T.J. (1993). Setting the agenda for gerontological nursing education. In C. Heine, (Ed.), *Determining the future of gerontological nursing education* (p. 11). New York: National League for Nursing Press.

[2] Waters, V. (Ed.). (1991). *Teaching gerontology: The curriculum imperative.* New York: National League for Nursing

[3] Carignan, A. (1991). The cognitive domain. In V. Waters (Ed.), *Teaching gerontology* (pp. 35-36)

[4] Small, N.R. (1993). Facilitating student learning: Effective teaching strategies are for baccalaureate education. In M. Burke & S. Sherman (Eds.), *Gerontological nursing: Issues and opportunities for the twenty-first century* (p. 64). New York: National League for Nursing Press.

[5] Roe, C. (1993). Kalamazoo Valley Community College. *Triton College Regional Dissemination Center Newsletter 3:* (1), 2.

[6] Small, N. ibid. p. 65.

[7] Tagliareni, E., Mengel, A., & Sherman, S. (1993). Parallel worlds of nursing practice. In *Ways of knowing and caring for the older adult.* New York: National League for Nursing Press.

Chapter 2

Experiential Learning Activities

The experiential learning activities included in this chapter fall into three categories. The first set includes activities designed to help in the understanding of normal aging and to develop new attitudes toward aging and the nursing of older people. The second assists students in the development of skills and attitudes needed in the care of the frail and dependent elderly. A third lists activities and cites additional print resources which can aid in the development of ethical reasoning and sensitivity in the care of older people.

Understanding Normal Aging and Developing New Attitudes

Given the negative societal attitudes toward the old and the chronically ill, on no topic in the curriculum does the faculty have greater interest in student attitudes than on the topic of gerontologic nursing. Learning activities that expose or alter the student's attitude toward the aging process are useful devices for initiating discussion. The Palmore quizzes, *Facts on Aging* Part 1, Part 2, and the Mental Health Quiz[8], are reproduced in a number of gerontology texts, as is the National Institute on Aging's *What is your aging IQ?*[9] Appendix D of *Teaching Gerontology* contains two learning activities that explore student feelings toward old age.[10]

7

As second generation project schools reported on their efforts to increase gerontologic nursing in their programs, the creativity of faculty became more noticeable. Sharon Souter, Program Director, and Will Anne Ricer, Instructor at New Mexico State University at Carlsbad, reported the following:

> One of the faculty, usually the program director, dresses up in the typical "stereo-type" of an elderly female. She sprays her hair silver, wears an ordinary waist dress, walks hunched over (uses a towel under her dress to make a hump-back), rolls her stockings, and uses a cane. Halloween makeup makes her appear to have many wrinkles. The program secretary escorts her down the hall; often students fail to recognize who she really is. Then she sits in front of the classroom and students take turns interviewing her on any subject from A to Z. The students then identify appropriate nursing diagnoses and do a simple teaching plan. At the end of the session the "old woman" reads the poem written by a woman patient who lived on a geriatric floor of Ashludie Hospital in Dunde, England, "What do you see, nurse, what do you see?" The impact on the class has continued to be dramatic as they do a self-evaluation of their view of the elderly.

> What do you see, nurse, what do you see?
> Are you thinking when you look at me—
> A crabbed old woman, not very wise,
> Uncertain of habit with faraway eyes.
> Who dribbles her food and makes no reply
> When you say in a loud voice, "I do wish you'd try."
> Who seems not to notice the things that you do
> And forever is losing a stocking or shoe.
> Who resisting or not, lets you do as you will
> With bathing and feeding, the long day to fill.
> Is that what you're thinking, is that what you see?
> Then open your eyes, nurse. You're not looking at me.

> I'll tell you who I am as I sit here so still.
> As I move at your bidding, eat at your will.
> I'm a small child of ten with a father and mother.
> Brothers and sisters who love one another;
> A young girl of sixteen with wings on her feet.
> Dreaming that soon a love she'll meet:
> A bride at twenty, my heart gives a leap,
> Remembering the vows that I promised to keep;
> At twenty-five now I have young of my own
> Who need me to build a secure, happy home.

A woman of thirty, my young now grow fast,
Bound together with ties that should last.
At forty my young sons have grown up and gone,
But my man's beside me to see I don't mourn.
At fifty once more babies play round my knee—
Again we know children, my loved one and me.
Dark days are upon me, my husband is dead.
I look at the future, I shudder with dread.
For my young are all rearing young of their own,
And I think of the years and the love that I've known.

I'm an old woman now and nature is cruel.
'Tis her jest to make old age look like a fool.
The body it crumbles, grace and vigor depart.
There is a stone where I once had a heart.
But inside this old carcass a young girl still dwells,
And now again my bittered heart swells.
I remember the joys, I remember the pain
And I'm loving and living life over again.
I think of the years, all too few, gone too fast,
And accept the stark fact that nothing can last.
So open your eyes, nurse, open and see
Not a crabbed old woman.
Look closer. See me!

We have learned that a number of teachers use this anonymous poem (the first line of which was used for the title of a widely-used video described in Chapter 4) to prompt discussion of attitudes toward older people. Beverly Clark at Jefferson Community College, NY, projects the *What Do You See, Nurse* verse and a second short poem onto a classroom screen. She has the students read the poems silently and write down their own feelings about aging, both of self and other family members. The poems are read aloud, and discussion follows. The second poem in this exercise is:

My grandpa went out walking
In his sneakers in the snow.
It mattered not how cold it was
Or where he meant to go.
He didn't believe in doctors,

Always had a better way.
He mixed and matched home remedies
While the rest of us would pray.
He did exactly as he pleased.
There was nothing we could do.
It's tough to win an argument
With a man who's 82.[11]

❑

At the Community College of Philadelphia, a student brought a Longfellow poem to class for a discussion associated with the well-elder experience which is part of the first semester at CCP (described in detail in *Teaching Gerontology*[12]). The poem has since become a regular part of a discussion about aging as a normal developmental sequence, meeting an objective held for the course to help students see aging and death in a continuum of life events rather than as fixed, chronological occurrences.

Nature
Henry Wadsworth Longfellow

As fond mother, when the day is o'er,
Leads by the hand her little child to bed,
Half willing, half reluctant to be led,
And leave his broken playthings on the floor
Still gazing at them through the open door,
Nor wholly reassured and comforted
By promises of others in their stead,
Which, though more splendid, may not please him more;
So Nature deals with us, and takes away
Our playthings one by one, and by the hand
Leads us to rest so gently, that we go
Scarce knowing if we wish to go or stay,
Being too full of sleep to understand
How far the unknown transcends the what we know.[13]

◻

Jenifer Gaydalo and Karen Wosiski at Burlington County College (NJ) use two Country Western songs to prompt discussion in clinical conferences during a nursing home rotation. They say that *Where've You Been,* by Kathy Mallere, "evokes tears and discussion concerning quality of life, love, and companionship." *All Dressed Up,* by Reba McIntyre, is used in pre-conference early in the rotation in combination with the short article, "Who Will Hug the Elderly." Wosiski reports she feels the conference assists students in looking beyond and beneath the physical appearance of residents and helps them incorporate *touch* into their care.

Who Will Hug the Elderly?
Patricia Conger Walsh, RN

From the moment of conception we are surrounded by touch. Tactile stimulation is imperative for normal infant growth and development. What calms a 2-year-old more effectively than the security of his parents' arms? The school-age child yearns for his mother's touch, but begins to develop his own sense of oneness and moves away. In the teen years, the meaning of touch changes as young men and women learn the joy of holding hands, kissing, and putting an arm around someone's shoulder. It shows you belong to someone.

As we mature and enter adulthood, we are no longer afraid to show our love by hugging or kissing. In sad times, a touch on the arm or a squeeze of the hand can lift a mountain of worries or grief. We express love and caring with a kiss, a hug, or an arm around the shoulder. Our most common greeting is a handshake, a joining of hands—again we touch. And, as we grow older, our children go off and share that touch with their own families; our siblings die, and then our spouses. Those who are still healthy can remain in the mainstream of life. But not all are so lucky. Some older people get sick, or confused. Many are lonely and isolated. After a lifetime of daily contact, suddenly it's gone. But it is still necessary to one's well-being. So the question becomes, "Who will hug the elderly?"

Many times I have brightened a mood, calmed the anxious, or helped orient the confused by gently touching an arm. As a nurse, I see many elderly people in hospitals or nursing homes who have few visitors. It's difficult to talk to a hard-of-hearing person, or to one who asks the same question over and over, but within that body lies a soul and heart of someone who loved, and gave, and right now needs. Hold her hand, give her a kiss, or put your arms around her and sing a song. No other intervention is more vital.

Often as I care for the elderly, they will reach up and touch my face or lay their hands on my arm; it's as if the touch makes things real again. As I help them out of bed, I have had patients ask, "Would you hug me?" It could be me there some day. And I wonder, will anyone hug me? I hope so. [14]

❑

At Weber State University, UT, students are given an opportunity to examine personal feelings about the words associated with the phenomenon of aging in a classroom activity developed by Karla Dalley.

Exercise
Personal Feelings About Terms Associated With Aging

Objective:
Students will explore their own attitudes about aging in our society.

Material Needed:
Blackboard and chalk
Room large enough for students to move around and stand in small groups
Five large signs with numbers and words printed as follows:
    1   MOST NEGATIVE
    2   NEGATIVE
    3   NEUTRAL
    4   POSITIVE
    5   MOST POSITIVE

Procedure:

Before class, post the five signs around the room. Allow at least 3 or 4 feet between signs. When class is assembled, ask the students to call out the words or phrases they associate with aging or old people in our society. Record them on the blackboard. Encourage them to think of both positive and negative terms, but do not discuss them at this time. Once you have a large list (about 5 minutes of brainstorming), ask the students to stand. Tell them you will call out the terms they have thought of one at a time in random order. Tell them that when they hear a word or phrase, they should go to the sign that most closely expresses the feeling the term invokes in them. Once they are clustered around the five signs, invite discussion from each group about their choice. Continue with other words or phrases until time alloted for this exercise is gone.

❏

At Ricks College, ID, Susan Garbett reports that since students initially hold such vastly diverse opinions about and experiences with the elderly,

> ...to help them think along similar lines, I usually begin my gerontology nursing course with an exercise which requires them to visualize themselves at age 85. The experience has them think about their desired environment, their social world, and their favorite activities. This approach fosters discussion of the realities of aging and brings the feelings of the elderly into focus for the students.

The directions and details of this activity are found in the book *Understanding Older Adults: An Experiential Approach to Learning* [15]. Several other activities are included in this book covering a variety of topics pertinent to the aged."

❏

Marilee Culhane at Triton College, IL, developed an exercise which she uses when students are interacting with elderly patients in any setting to prompt them to focus on positive qualities and characteristics in the older person. She finds the exercise helps students see older people differently. She developed the list in an interesting way: she went into a Triton-sponsored special class for seniors, and asked the men and women present to make a list of things they liked best about themselves. Their responses became the Experiential Exercise.

TRITON COLLEGE
NURSING PROGRAM

Experiential Exercise: Things That I Like About an Older Adult

Check ✔ descriptions that apply:

Loving
Slender
Strong religious faith
Intelligent
Positive influence on family
Versatile
Accepts people
Stylish dresser
Loves children
Enthusiastic
Human
Responsible
Appreciates nature
Kind
Openness
Tackles new jobs
Eager to learn
Insightful
Good posture
Resourceful
Values relationships
Hard worker
Very perceptive
Eccentric
Witty
Pleased with appearance
Thrifty
Positive outlook
Reads
Calm
Mentors others
Good homemaker
Curious
Confident
Enjoys sleeping
Good speller
Satisfied with life
Loyal
Ability to concentrate
Regular exercise

Keeps confidences
Able to talk about feelings
Hair
Seeks help
Spontaneous
Travel experiences
Polite
Ability to laugh
Reliable
Active in groups
Musical talent
Emotionally strong
Sports fan
Trusting
Good seamstress
Problem solver
Likes self
Informed on current events
Meticulous
Good friend
Well-organized
Financial support
Affectionate
Eyes
Sexy
Babysitter
Sensitive
Loves animals
Content
Caregiver
Sincere
Knows limitations and
     strengths
Good elimination
Generous with time
Curious
Listens well
Creative
Trustworthy
Poised

An easy smile
Friendly
Loves to cook
Attractive
Good dancer
Common sense
Articulate
Soft-spoken
Alive
Interesting story teller
Adaptive
Tells it like it is
Calm
Outgoing
Leader
Practical
Honest
Easygoing
Pleasant
Neat
Craft ability
Enjoys life
No wrinkles
Not judgmental
Pride in family
Natural cheerfulness
Enjoys flowers
Good converser
Initiative
Easy to talk to
Personality
Forgives easily
Historian in family
Fingernails
Incurable optimist
Sweet
Listens to music
Rich
Enjoys eating out
Can entertain self

List 10 you like best.

1. _____
2. _____
3. _____
4. _____
5. _____
6. _____
7. _____
8. _____
9. _____
10. _____

List 4 you want to develop.

1. _____
2. _____
3. _____
4. _____

Now you can develop these qualities
for the older adult you will become.

Shoreline Community College, WA, also assigns students to a longitudinal one-on-one experience with an older adult living in a retirement residence or in an assisted living facility. This assignment is concurrent with a course entitled *Nursing Practice and Psychosocial Disturbances,* and provides students with the opportunity to examine concepts of psychosocial nursing and psychopathology to people in elder-care settings. We have included several components of the assignment, developed by Ann Ross and Janice R. Ellis of the Shoreline faculty: Nursing 112 Course Description, Guidelines When Working With Clients, Documentation of Visits, Letter to Resident, and Resident Evaluation of Experience with Student.

NURSING 112 COURSE DESCRIPTION
SHORELINE COMMUNITY COLLEGE

Nursing 112: Nursing Practice and Psychosocial Disturbances Practicum

Course Description:
This course is taken concurrently with Nursing 102 Nursing Practice and Psychosocial Disturbances and provides the opportunity to apply concepts of psychosocial nursing and psychopathology to the care of persons in a variety of settings. The focus includes:
1. Establishing a long-term relationship with a specified client to assist that client in dealing with activities of daily living or life span transitions.
2. Establishing short-term relationships with clients in groups to assist them in meeting emotional, behavioral, and mental health needs and enhance skills of daily living.

Gerontology Practicum Experience:
Clients for this experience reside in retirement residences or assisted living facilities. Individual clients are selected by social service or nursing personnel in the agency who understand the experience and believe that the older adult would benefit from a 1:1 relationship.

One faculty member is assigned the responsibility for coordinating all gerontology client experiences including contact with facilities, orientation, and assignment of students to clients. This person is also the resource/problem-solver for the experience.

Each student is also assigned to a 6 hour practicum group supervised on site by an instructor in the course. All course faculty include discussion of gerontology client relationships and experiences in post-clinical conferences at the group practitum. Weekly LOGs that document experiences, activities, and meeting of objectives in the gerontology experience are submitted to the instructor of this group practicum.

Meetings with the resident are as follows:

a. **Week 1**

Orientation for all students at the designated time. Students contact resident during this week after the orientation; introduce self, and arrange for a regular meeting time. This is to be a specifically designated time and must be acceptable to both the student and the resident.

b. **Week 2**

Students are to become acquainted with the resident. Topics of conversation might include:

- The resident's story of his or her life as experienced by the resident (often called "life review").
- Events that are occurring, are newsworthy, or of interest to the resident.
- Health promotion (e.g. exploring what the resident does or can do to promote personal health and well-being).
- Health maintenance (e.g. in discussing the resident's management of a chronic disease including medications taken and other health care measures, students must be careful that they do not give advice about areas that they have not yet studied. It is helpful to let the resident know the student is interested in the resident's concerns and is willing to assist the resident to find ways through facility avenues to deal with the concern).

Students will begin accumulating data through conversation but are not to ask intrusive questions or deeply personal data of the resident.

Students are to begin identifying activities that will support the resident's psychosocial needs and enhance the interactions with and assessments of the resident.

c. **Weeks 3-9**

Students will:

- Continue with the relationship.

- Plan activities approximately two weeks in advance. Engage in activities and continue to expand and enlarge the database regarding this resident through observation, listening skills, and the use of non-intrusive, non-directive communication techniques.
- Adapt planned activities to better meet the resident's needs as more is learned.
- Include planning for termination as part of the relationship.
  d. **Week 10**
  Last meeting and termination of the relationship.

Written Assignments:
  a. Each visit is documented with an entry on the page "Documentation of Visits" for Gerontology clients. Include:
  - Date of visit.
  - Time of visit (beginning to end).
  - List of activities engaged in with resident.
  - A **very brief** description of the interaction and activities that occurred.
  - Activities planned for the following week.
  b. Entries in the weekly log that describe the visit with the resident, activities of the student and resident, resident's responses and concerns. Include objectives for practicum that were met through the experience. See "Directions for Log."
  c. A client summary is due in completed form by Week 10. A draft must be prepared and approved by the practicum instructor by Week 8 or 9; the final summary must be typed on the form provided in the syllabus and submitted to the instructor by Week 10.

SHORELINE COMMUNITY COLLEGE

Guidelines When Working With Clients

Assigned (1:1) Clients
  Purpose:
  To work with one individual for an extended period of time, from several weeks to the entire quarter, depending on client availability.
  a. Goals for the client
  To:
  - Increase the sense of trust.
  - Develop/enhance skills for living.
  - Enhance the individual's self-esteem.

- Increase ability to relate to others.
- Focus on the "here-and-now" and adaptation to change.

b. Goals for the student

To:

- Increase observational skills and interviewing techniques to enhance data collection.
- Develop facilitative communication skills.
- Intervene in scientific and therapeutic ways with the client/patient to assist the person in meeting his/her psychosocial needs. e.g. experiencing life reviews, adapting to changing life and health status.
- Increase knowledge of the wellness-illness continuum focusing on wellness and client strengths.

SHORELINE COMMUNITY COLLEGE Nursing 112 Documentation of Visits/ Gerontology Client	Student _____ Quarter/Year _____ Facility _____

Day/ Date	Times of Visit	Activities with Client Concerns/Questions for Instructor	Plans for Next Two Visits

SHORELINE COMMUNITY COLLEGE

Nursing Program

To: Resident
From: Ann Ross, Professor of Nursing

The nursing faculty believe our nursing students would benefit from having a quarter long contact with an older person. The time involvement is approximately one hour per week for nine weeks. This experience assists the student to have a better understanding of your age group by hearing about the concerns you have about changes in your life and hearing your perspectives on ways you have lived your life.

Not only might you be the one who could help the student in these areas, you might also enjoy the opportunity to participate in the education of future health care professionals.

Through this experience, the student can offer the residents who participate the following: 1) a listener, 2) assistance in looking at some of the resident's health concerns, and 3) some ideas regarding the health system.

Some activities the two of you could do during your time together could include: sitting and talking, looking at photo albums and remembrances, playing cards or table games, talking walks, or doing a project together.

You will be contacted by your facility staff regarding your willingness to participate in this endeavor. If you agree, and are assigned a nursing student, students will begin their quarter with an orientation to the facility during the week of March 29, 1993. That week they may meet you in person or by phone to set a time to see you for the remainder of the quarter.

The students are supervised by an instructor at the college; the facility staff serve as a liaison in the facility.

The following policies apply to the student's experience:

The students cannot take the residents in the student's car or go places with the resident's (or resident's family or friend's) car.

The students are not to have meals with residents.

The students are not to receive or give gifts.

The students is to meet at the same time and day as initially agreed by student and resident together. If circumstances require rescheduling, the two may plan for an alternate time.

Thank you for considering participating in this experience.

SHORELINE COMMUNITY COLLEGE

To: Shoreline Community Resident
From: Nursing 102 Faculty

We want to thank you for participating in a relationship with a nursing student for this past term.

At this time, we would appreciate hearing from you about this experience. If you wish to respond, please answer the questions below and return this letter to us in the enclosed, stamped, addressed envelope. All replies are kept private.

1. Based on a scale of 0 to 6, please mark on the line your overall opinion of this experience.

0 ------------ 1 -------------- 2 ------------- 3 ------------- 4 -------------- 5 ------------ 6

Very   Very
Negative   Positive

2. Would you be willing to have another nursing student assigned to you?

   Yes ___ No ___ (If no, we would appreciate knowing your reason.)

3. Any suggestions you have for making future student-resident relationships better would be appreciated.

4. If you would like to speak personally with an instructor about the experience, we would be glad to give you a telephone call. Indicate here:

   Please call me ___ Name _____

   Telephone number _____

   You do not need to include your name if you would rather not do so. You may call us if you prefer:

   Ann Ross, RN, 546-4708
   Janice Ellis, RN, 546-4756

   (Note: Instructors will not be available from June 11, 1993 to September 28, 1993.)

❏

Learning About Nursing of Frail, Dependent Elders

Faculty who inaugurate second-level clinical instruction in a nursing home soon realize that the teaching strategies and organization of learning activities for students need to be different in the nursing home than in acute care facilities.[16] New learning activities and assignments have been designed and implemented as faculty sought ways to formulate for students a perspective on the nursing of elderly patients that transcends setting. Classroom activities, also, have moved away from the traditional diseases-of-aging-and-nursing-responses lecture. Both project school faculty and their colleagues in the second generation schools have developed new learning activities for both clinical and classroom experience. In this section, suggestions are made and formats presented for the use of journals and other personal, written accounts of clinical experiences, for the use of case studies as a teaching method, and other classroom and clinical laboratory learning experiences.

Journals, diaries, or clinical logs are used by a number of programs to encourage students to reflect on their experiences with frail, dependent elders. Delores Nelson at Gannon University, PA, is a strong advocate of clinical journal writing as a learning activity. She observes that "...because of emphasis on technical aspects of care in health settings, nursing students often are underprepared to deal with personal concerns and sensitive issues in the course of their clinical day. Yet, nursing students deal with a variety of sensitive and often stressful situations involving elderly clients....Written, active dialogue in the form of journal writing between a nursing instructor and a student provides a means for developing professional thinking... . It is a shared experience that can foster self-development in the clinical learning experience and the transition from novice toward expert." As used by Nelson, the students are encouraged to write at least one page at the end of the clinical day reflecting on their clinical experience. She reports that students say the "journal writing helps them to 'reflect back on what [they] had done right and what [they] could do better' and to 'help organize [their] thoughts and feel better about various situations that occur.' From the clinical instructor's point of view it provides feedback and information on sensitive issues that students are dealing with but reluctant to discuss in the group situation during post-clinical conferences." Following are the guidelines which Nelson gives her students, along with the five references she recommends for faculty who wish to explore the use of this teaching technique.

GANNON UNIVERSITY
NURSING PROGRAM
Written Journal Guidelines

Log or "Sketchbook" of Clinical Activities
Write or type out a running list or narrative of the activities that you are involved in during your clinical day. This can be brief sentences or even phrases. (Don't worry about grammar or spelling; it's your free flow of thoughts that count.) This should be done during the clinical day or at least at the end of the day before you leave so that you don't forget particularly important activities.

Critical Incident
When you have completed the log or "sketchbook" of clinical activities, choose one *critical incident,* activity, special event, or situation that stands out or highlights your day as you work with your elderly client. Consider the following questions as you describe the incident:

- What is happening at the time of this *critical incident* or activity (subjective and objective data)? Be as descriptive as you can.
- What are you thinking, feeling, and/or doing at this time?
- What is it about this *critical incident* or activity that makes it stand out for you during the clinical day?

This *critical incident* writing should be done at the end of your clinical day or as soon as possible before you get involved in other personal activities away from the nursing care setting. It will probably take about 30-45 minutes of your time (give it at least 15-20 minutes) and be 2-3 pages, depending on your writing or typing. There arc no page limits.

References for Faculty

Fulwiler, T. (1982). The personal connection: Journal writing across the curriculum. In R. Fulwiler & A. Young (Eds.), *Language connections: Writing and reading across the curriculum.* Chicago, IL: National Council of Teachers of English.

Hahnemann, B. (1986). Journal writing: A key to promoting critical thinking in nursing students. *Journal of Nursing Education, 25* (5), 213-215.

Holly, M. L. (1984). *Keeping a personal-professional journal.* Victoria, Australia: Deakin University Press.

Holly, M. L. (1989). *Writing to growing: Keeping a personal-professional journal.* Portsmouth, NH: Heinemann Educational Books.

Wolf, M. (1989). Journal writing: A means to an end in training students to work with older adults. Chicago, IL: Paper presented at the 14th Annual Meeting of the Association for Gerontology in Higher Education.

❏

At Howard Community College, MD, Cherry Rappaport asks students to make entries in a journal each clinical day they spend in a nursing home. Students are placed in the nursing home during their first semester and then again in the fourth semester; the first semester clinical focuses on communication with elders. In an assignment entitled "Reflections on the Use of Self," Rappaport asks students to respond to these questions:

- Describe your behavior/thoughts/feelings in working with your elderly patients. What was it like when you were with your patient this morning?
- Assess the consequences of your thoughts in the patient care setting. How do my thoughts influence my care in the long term care setting? Describe an example of genuineness.

Community College of Philadelphia faculty "utilize logs as a tool to facilitate dialogue about issues of concern to students and to encourage students to explore subtle meanings when providing nursing care to residents," according to Eileen Weik, clinical faculty at CCP. She notes that sometimes faculty ask students to address specific questions, and cites two examples:

- If you were your resident, what would you want from your nurse today?
- How would those needs be different in acute care?

❑

Andrea Mengel, also from CCP, designed a learning activity for a post-conference in which students examine a particular issue in elder care in relation to a particular nursing home resident in preparation. The worksheet she prepares for students follows.

COMMUNITY COLLEGE OF PHILADELPHIA
DEPARTMENT OF NURSING

NAME _____

Nursing Home Clinical:
Learning Activity:
The following questions will be discussed at post-conference during Week IV.

From your clinical experience in the nursing home, describe two situations in which a resident's autonomy or independence needs were an issue and how these were addressed.

    1. Issue:

       How addressed:

2. Issue:

How addressed:

Consider these two situations. Describe three factors which influenced how these situations were addressed.

1.

2.

3.

Would you have handled these two situations differently? If so, how:

1.

2.

Define autonomy or independence in your own words.

Is autonomy or independence a realistic goal for the nursing home resident? Explain your position.

Communication techniques are a staple ingredient in every nursing curriculum. With the rise in conscious attention to preparing students to work with an aging population, many faculty are adding didactic and clinical attention to communication with elders who manifest alterations in communication abilities. At Weber State University, UT, the Feil method for communicating with disoriented elders called "validation technique" is taught to students. Instructor Colleen Brill describes the Feil approach as using "empathy and respect to validate the disoriented person's internal reality instead of focusing on frustrating and often in-effective exchanges directed toward function and communication in the 'real' world." She suggests that students can be taught validation techniques in a fundamentals nursing course, a management course in a long-term care setting, or in a mental health nursing course using long-term care clinical settings. At Weber the students participate in a one hour seminar devoted to validation techniques prior to entering the long-term care setting, including video tapes and computer programs developed by Brill and colleagues. For further information, Brill recommends the following resources:

Brill, C. (Producer). (1992). *Validation techniques in long term care* [Videotape]. Ogden, UT: Weber State University.

Brill, C., Castleton, M., & Hess, M. L. (1993). *Validation techniques* [Computer program]. Ogden, UT: Weber State University.

Feil, N. (1992). *V/F validation: The Feil method* (3rd ed.). Cleveland, OH: Edward Feil Productions

❑

People Search is a format for designing a classroom activity that Joan Libner, Triton College, IL, found outlined in *Blueprints for Thinking in the Cooperative Classroom*.[17] She has created *People Search* activities on several topics—for example, diabetes and cardiac care—which she uses as an introduction to a course or a unit of study, or as a tool for review of a unit of study. She and Mary Ellen Simmons have used the *People Search* format as an icebreaker at faculty development workshops and meetings. Libner developed a classroom activity in this format to introduce Triton students to a nursing home experience in the third semester of their ADN program, and entitled it "Getting Older and Better." She explains how it is used:

> *Each member of the class (group) receives a copy of the* People Search. *Each person is to find individuals who can truthfully sign each statement. Only one statement can be signed per person per sheet, although a person may sign a different statement on another individual's sheet. Not only does one ask for a signature from another person, but the two must discuss the answer.*

When the signing process is completed, the group leader calls on individuals and asks who signed the first statement. When that person's name is given, the leader then asks the signer to discuss his/her response or experience with that topic. Or the entire group of people who signed any one statement may be asked to discuss their responses.[17]

Getting Older and Better

Find Someone Who:

Knows an aging person.

Has a family member living in a nursing home.

Has ever worked in a nursing home.

Can describe a positive aspect of aging.

Can predict what the elderly population will be like in the year 2010.

Can describe a physical change normally associated with aging.

Has signed an advance directive form.

Can describe what OBRA regulations mean to the RN in the nursing home setting.

Can name three differences in working as a registered nurse in a nursing home compared to working in a hospital.

Can describe what they hope to be like at age 80.

In the fourth semester of the ADN program at Front Range Community College, CO, Dr. Alma Mueller, Nursing Department Chair, has developed a set of activities which introduce students to the nursing home clinical experience.

FRONT RANGE COMMUNITY COLLEGE, WESTMINSTER CAMPUS WESTMINSTER, COLORADO

Approaches to Nursing Home Clinical Learning in the Last Semester of an ADN Program

Immediately prior to the nursing home clinical experience in the fourth semester, the students attend a seminar. The purpose of this seminar is to help prepare them for their nursing home experience. It includes:

1. A presentation on "The RN in Long-Term Care."

   This presentation focuses on changes in long term care, the impact RNs can have in long term care and on the challenge of the long-term relationship.

2. Small group discussions on feelings and roles related to long term care.

   A feelings questionnaire about responding to the impaired elderly (tool attached) is completed and discussed.
   The students compare the role of the RN in long-term versus acute-care settings.

3. Information on assessments (Minimum Data Set) and reimbursement in long-term care.

In addition to this seminar, four other activities have been incorporated successfully into the nursing home experience. These activities are:

Prose or Poem on Aging
During the clinical experience at the nursing home, each student writes an essay or poem on the topic "Aging: What it means to me." The purpose of this is to help the student formulate her or his own thoughts on the meaning that growing old has for them individually. We receive some extremely meaningful and poetic works from this exercise. Students also often comment on what an excellent learning experience the assignment proved to be.

Simulating a Disability

During a nursing home post conference, the students participate in an exercise simulating a disability. This exercise occurs after the students have worked with the residents for at least two days.

Students have indicated to us that they truly start feeling the restrictions of the disability after "having" the disability for about 20-30 minutes. They have indicated that they have a better understanding of the elderly resident after the experience, and gain a lot from the opportunity to discuss pertinent issues relating to the elderly which are on the tool.

The tool and its explanation follow this discussion.

Remotivation Therapy

The third activity is one which incorporates psychiatric principles and skills into the nursing home experience. Our students do not conduct group sessions with patients in psychiatric nursing. However, the nursing home experience provides an appropriate place for them to conduct group sessions based on Remotivation Therapy. This therapy was first developed by a nurse, bringing together residents who have cognitive impairment and pushing them to speak from their more "well" areas.

The students review the article: "Stimulation Through Remotivation," by Glee Gamble Lyon, *American Journal of Nursing*, May 1971.

While this is an older article, the principles of Remotivation Therapy have not changed. Additionally, this article describes the therapy in such a way that students can immediately practice it. Student creativity is set into high gear as evidenced by some of the inventive sessions they have conducted.

Attitudinal Survey

The fourth activity is a discussion of attitudes the students have toward the nursing role in long-term care and toward elderly residents. An attitudinal survey is completed individually by each student. The students then discuss their perceptions and those of other nurses and society. This activity helps them examine their own biases and assess the realities of nursing home interventions. The tool follows.

FRONT RANGE COMMUNITY COLLEGE, WESTMINSTER CAMPUS

Attitudinal Survey on Gerontological Nursing

Circle your first reaction to each of the following statements. Only you will see your responses.

Upon being introduced to the 64-year-old CEO of a hospital, I would call him by his first name.

STRONGLY AGREE　　　AGREE　　　NEUTRAL　　　DISAGREE　　　STRONGLY DISAGREE

Upon introducing myself to a 64-year-old resident at the nursing home for the first time, I would call him by his first name.

STRONGLY AGREE　　　AGREE　　　NEUTRAL　　　DISAGREE　　　STRONGLY DISAGREE

The elderly prefer being called by "affectionate" terms such as Honey, Sweetie, Pops, Gram, Sugar, etc.

STRONGLY AGREE　　　AGREE　　　NEUTRAL　　　DISAGREE　　　STRONGLY DISAGREE

The concept of high level wellness is NOT as critical in gerontological nursing.

STRONGLY AGREE　　　AGREE　　　NEUTRAL　　　DISAGREE　　　STRONGLY DISAGREE

The nursing shortage is over if there are very low vacancy rates for RNs in hospitals (not a great demand for RNs in acute care).

STRONGLY AGREE　　　AGREE　　　NEUTRAL　　　DISAGREE　　　STRONGLY DISAGREE

Nursing home nurses should get no experience credit for nursing home practice when they switch to hospital nursing.

STRONGLY AGREE　　　AGREE　　　NEUTRAL　　　DISAGREE　　　STRONGLY DISAGREE

Acute care nurses should get no experience credit for hospital practice when they switch to nursing home work.

STRONGLY AGREE　　　AGREE　　　NEUTRAL　　　DISAGREE　　　STRONGLY DISAGREE

Clinical experience for student nurses in acute care hospitals is adequate preparation for gerontological nursing practice.

STRONGLY AGREE　　　AGREE　　　NEUTRAL　　　DISAGREE　　　STRONGLY DISAGREE

Acute care nurses should earn more pay than nursing home nurses.

STRONGLY AGREE　　　AGREE　　　NEUTRAL　　　DISAGREE　　　STRONGLY DISAGREE

Hospital nurses need better assessment skills than nursing home nurses.

STRONGLY AGREE　　　AGREE　　　NEUTRAL　　　DISAGREE　　　STRONGLY DISAGREE

I would never work in a nursing home.

STRONGLY AGREE　　　AGREE　　　NEUTRAL　　　DISAGREE　　　STRONGLY DISAGREE

I would never work in a nursing home unless I learned more about gerontological nursing and RN roles and responsibilities there.

STRONGLY AGREE　　　AGREE　　　NEUTRAL　　　DISAGREE　　　STRONGLY DISAGREE

CREATIVE APPROACHES
TO AGING AND MENTAL HEALTH

Responding to the Impaired Elderly

Dr. Theodore H. Koff
Denver, Colorado

Please respond to the following questions using the key as follows:

1. = Strongly Agree	3. = Disagree
2. = Agree	4 = Totally Disagree

_____ 1. Disintegration of the family is the cause of many of the losses of old age.

_____ 2. Active minds and body forestall mental impairments.

_____ 3. Most older people do not know they are impaired.

_____ 4. Loss of memory runs in the family.

_____ 5. It is wasteful to invest time with mentally impaired people if it keeps us from preventing losses of the more able.

_____ 6. If it is painful for families to visit the mentally impaired, they should not be pushed.

_____ 7. Often, the best response to the older person is tender loving care.

_____ 8. If you don't have a good psychiatrist it is difficult to adequately serve the mentally impaired.

_____ 9. If we live long enough, we all will show signs of mental malfunction.

_____ 10. Often, the most humane treatment of agitated behavior is drug therapy.

_____ 11. Well people should not be disturbed by the impaired.

_____ 12. Restraints are often a necessity to prevent the impaired person from hurting him/herself.

_____ 13. Bowel and bladder control can be taught.

_____ 14. As people age they begin to experience losses in terms of friends or relatives and often substitute objects for people.

_____ 15. Nothing can be done for the older person once he/she is confused.

_____ 16. Time between memory loss and death is often quite short.

_____ 17. There is a better return on money spent for the young than for the old.

_____ 18. The institution is better prepared to serve the mentally impaired than is the family or home.

_____ 19. All people are equal in the eyes of God.

_____ 20. I hope that I will die before I become mentally impaired.

FRONT RANGE COMMUNITY COLLEGE, WESTMINSTER CAMPUS
NUR 217: Comprehensive Nursing of Older Adults

A Personal Look at Aging With a Disability
A Personal Look at Death

Each student will bring aids to create a disability for him or herself during the 50-minute discussion. You must keep your "disability" for at least 50 minutes in order to feel confined. Some suggestions for the "disability" are listed but you may create your own. Use your imagination: Blindness (bring a blindfold), a speech impediment (tape mouth so you cannot speak), a stroke (tie one arm and leg on same side to chair so you cannot move them), lower paralysis (tie both legs to legs of chair so you cannot move), severe upper arm arthritis (tie both arms behind back).

QUESTIONS FOR DISCUSSION: Use the following questions as discussion guidelines for a 50-minute discussion while each student has his/her disability. Then spend 10 minutes after removing the disability discussing feelings and insights gained by the "disability" experience.

YOU ARE 75 YEARS OLD AND HAVE ALZHEIMERS....

1. Would your family be able to afford a nursing home? If not, who would be taking care of you?
2. If you were in a nursing home, would you want your family to visit you? How often and for how long a visit?
3. What qualities would you want your nurse/nursing care assistant/care giver to possess?
4. In the final stage of the disease when death comes usually in the form of pneumonia, would you want antibiotics?
5. Would you choose suicide if you could get it done, and if so, at what point?

YOU ARE 72 YEARS OLD AND HAVE A PHYSICAL DISABILITY... (Multiple Sclerosis, severe crippling arthritis, a disabling stroke, paralysis, Parkinson's, etc.)

1. Would your family be able to afford a nursing home? If not, who would be taking care of you?
2. If you were in a nursing home, would you want your family to visit you? How often and for how long a visit?
3. What qualities would you want your nurse/nursing assistant/care giver to possess?
4. Would you choose suicide if you could get it done, and if so at what point?

YOU HAVE JUST BEEN TOLD THAT YOU HAVE ONE MONTH TO LIVE (3 WEEKS AT HOME AND THE LAST WEEK IN THE HOSPITAL).
1. Who will you tell and who will you not tell and why?
2. Is there anyone you want to have a reconciliation with?
3. What "loose ends" will you tie up?
4. What regrets do you have?
5. Would you choose to die at home?

WHILE IN THE HOSPITAL:
1. You are in pain. Do you want liberal pain medication or not, and do you want control over your pain medication or not?
2. Visitors: limited? who?
3. Describe the nurse you want, and his/her qualities. Would you want yourself as your nurse? How often would you want the nurse to visit?
4. Do you want your family to be present when you die?
5. Do you want to have measures such as IV, NG, antibiotics, respirator to possibly prolong your life?

NOW GO BACK AND ANSWER THE ABOVE TWO SETS OF QUESTIONS ABOUT DYING AS THOUGH YOU ARE 80 YEARS OLD. FOR QUESTION NUMBER 5 IN THE FIRST GROUP, IF YOU WERE IN A NURSING HOME, WOULD YOU WANT TO DIE IN THE NURSING HOME OR IN THE HOSPITAL?

❏

Jodie Freeland at St. Elizabeth Hospital/St. Joseph College, IN, has developed a learning activity designed to help students gain a perspective on nursing home placement from the point of view of the family and the prospective resident seeking placement. In Jodie Freeland's words:

> The purpose of the exercise is three-fold: to increase student awareness of the difficult task of selecting a long-term care facility, to increase the student's ability to help with discharge planning, and to increase student empathy when the family and patient are faced with choosing a facility.

> Before the students come to class they should have read at least two references regarding nursing home placement from the consumer perspective. The two in our library that the students usually read are both published in 1984 by the American Health Care Association (1201 L Street, N.W., Washington, DC 20005): Thinking About A Nursing Home: A Consumer's Guide for Choosing a Long Term Care Facility, and Here's Help! How Do I Pay For Nursing Home Care?

> At the beginning of the class I have the students list concepts that need to be considered when evaluating nursing homes. I want answers that include location, ethnic, cultural, and religious beliefs, nurse/patient ratio, social activities, special rehabilitation services, medical staff, appearance of the food, fire/environmental safety, and financial arrangements.

> After this discussion I divide the class into nursing home representatives and customers. Depending on the size of the class, each care facility has either 2 or 3 representatives. The remainder of the class is divided into customer pairs. The object of the representatives is to sell their facility and attract the largest number of clients. The object of the pairs is to find a facility that best meets the needs of their situation. The pairs visit each facility, ask questions, gather data, and select a facility.

> The simulation concludes with discussion of their experiences. The pairs state their choice of a nursing home, and, most important, their reasons for that decision.

Jodie Freeland has developed five nursing home facility profiles: State Home, St. Peter's Nursing Home, Live-Again Grand Lodge, Carefree Nursing Home, and Poer Manor. One is included here to illustrate Freeland's approach; the reader who intends to try this exercise will want to develop his or her own profiles reflecting the community in which students live and work. Freeland notes that prior to beginning the exercise, facility representatives may and usually do add more details and features to the sketchy profile which she has developed to start them out.

Carefree Nursing Home

Carefree Nursing Home is licensed as a comprehensive care facility and certified intermediate care for Medicaid patients. It is a not-for-profit community-owned facility, dedicated to the promotion of the physical, mental, and spiritual well-being of its residents. Located in a rural area, it has a 96 bed capacity, is single-storied, and air conditioned. It has a double alarm safety system for wandering residents. The building is of modern design and meets all safety codes; it is fully sprinkled and has smoke detectors. It is accessible for handicapped and features spacious lounges and activity areas.

The facility provides top quality care at reasonable cost. The following services are included in the basic rate: nursing care, room, regular and therapeutic diets, routine supplies, activities, social service, a volunteer program, open visiting, personal laundry, and whirlpool baths. Other services which are available include physician visits, pharmacy services, laboratory work, therapies, beauty and barber services, meals to visitors, in-room phone service, and transportation to clinics.

❑

Case studies have long been used as a learning activity in nursing. At the Community College of Philadelphia (CCP), the case study method has become increasingly compelling as a way to help students individualize the care of older patients, and to see the patient or resident in a whole-life perspective. Elaine Tagliareni at CCP introduced the use of a drawn-from-life case study over the course of the entire semester. She believes case studies based on real people and their real life events are more effective as learning activities than imaginary situations. In our contemporary world, there is no shortage of case examples of life as an older adult. For nursing educators, many of whom are in mid-life, there are aging relatives and friends who are coping with typical late-life health and care concerns. Clients that students meet during a well-elder experience can be another source of likely case material.

At the Community College of Philadelphia, the topic of gerontologic nursing begins in the first semester with a health maintenance focus in the fundamentals of nursing course. For the student, the point of view that optimal function in a safe environment is the desired nursing outcome is presented as a base for their learning experiences in the "well-elder" assignment and the acute-hospital setting.

The fundamentals of nursing case study concerns two aging sisters, who were, in fact, the great aunts of a faculty member. Both sisters had chronic health problems which, in the course of the study, triggered episodes of hospitalization and rehabilitation. The case is introduced early in the semester, with the 83 and 72 year old sisters defined as healthy, independent older adults with chronic health problems. Each week new case events are given to the student, correlated with other subject matter presentations and discussion topics. Health-related events in the lives of the sisters unfold over the course of the semester, giving the students an opportunity for reflection, which is itself a method of learning. Josephina and Angelina come alive again each semester for every successive student group as they provide a point of convergence for discussion of comfort, pain management, prevention of infection, teaching-learning, and communication. The overarching topic in the serialized case study is health maintenance. With weekly discussion and planning of care, the two aging sisters assume a reality which appears to be an effective guide to student thought and action. Henry, a CCP early semester student, wrote in his clinical log, "I was really nervous about taking care of my own patient this week. When I entered the room I found an 82 year old woman who looked really sick. Her sister was with her, feeding her breakfast. When I started her bath, she told me to make sure that I kept her good and warm because 'it is freezing in this place.' I thought to myself, 'Hey! Wait a minute. I can do this; it's Josephine!"

The fourth semester objectives at Community College of Philadelphia have been shaped by the faculty's experience in the nursing home project and are intended to assist students to understand and appreciate the complexities of nursing care in both the acute- and long-term care settings. Students are expected to develop a personal (professional) perspective on care of older adults grounded in the knowledge that curative care has its limitations, and that the special needs of the older adult more often involve function and connectedness in a safe and familiar environment. The following case study is used as a basis for analysis and discussion during that semester:

COMMUNITY COLLEGE OF PHILADELPHIA
DEPARTMENT OF NURSING

CASE STUDY: MARY

Mary, a 76 year old Spanish speaking woman originally from Puerto Rico, has been a resident of Cedar Brook Nursing Home for the past two years. Previously, she lived with her daughter, son-in-law and 7 grandchildren in a row house in West Philadelphia. She came to the U.S. fifty years ago as a widow and raised her two children by herself, working as a cleaning person at night in a center city high-rise. Mary understands English but speaks the language haltingly.

Three years ago, Mary fell and broke her right hip; after a lengthy hospitalization she became confused and agitated and began to accuse her daughter and son-in-law of stealing her furniture. Occasionally, she expressed a belief that "they" (daughter and son-in-law) were trying to poison her. Because Mary's daughter worked outside the home, she placed her at Cedar Brook.

When Mary arrived two years ago at the nursing home, she became a "favorite." Her agitation decreased: she was maintained on Haldol 1mg qHS. Mary talked to everyone, continually, in both Spanish and English. She kept her room meticulously tidy and always cleaned all the tables in the dining room after meals. Her cognitive function remained stable, with difficulty only in immediate recall and recognition, as well as poor time orientation.

Six months ago, Mary's daughter took her home for a trial period. However, Mary was left alone for long intervals. Unfortunately, while left alone one day, Mary forgot about a pot on the stove and almost started a fire. Mary's daughter realized that she could not handle Mary at home.

Upon readmission to the nursing home, Mary's agitation was markedly increased. She paced continuously, sleeping only for brief intervals within a 24 hour period. She would walk the halls, mumbling to herself and when approached and greeted by the nursing staff, evidenced no eye contact. She rummaged through her room, tearing pieces of toilet paper from the roll and carefully folding them into neat little piles. Then she would repeat the process over and over. Mary ate very little and rarely sat at her dining room place for meals. Sometimes she cried, silently, as she paced and mumbled.

The physician ordered an increase in Haldol to 2mg BID and Halcion at HS. After three weeks, Mary evidenced only minimal improvement. The nursing staff suggested treating Mary for her "manicky" type behaviors.

1. Describe the behaviors exhibited by Mary. What do they indicate to you? Would you have made the same suggestion?

The nursing staff met with the health care team to design a new care plan for Mary. They suggested that Mary be placed on Tegretol, not Lithium, since the nursing staff were concerned about maintaining adequate fluid and Na+ intake, due to her severe hyperactivity.

2. Explain the nursing staff's rationale. How do fluids and Na+ intake relate to maintenance of therapeutic Lithium levels?

3. If you were at the care conference, what outcome criteria would you suggest for Mary now? Prioritize.

After six weeks on Tegretol, Mary showed minimal improvement. Her pacing decreased at bedtime, probably due to her fatigue and weakness and to the fact that the nursing assistants initiated a bed-time ritual of a hot bath and hot soup (this had been Mary's practice at home). Mary also received Ativan at bedtime. But Mary continued to evidence extensive compulsive behaviors and rarely sat for meals. Her weight dropped 4 pounds. She cried impulsively throughout the day, moaning and wringing her hands. She also was severely constipated. Sometimes, she talked about her daughter, who visited regularly, as "evil" and the "poison-woman." She said an angel told her she would die soon.

The nursing staff requested another psych evaluation. After consultation with the nursing staff and interviews with Mary, the psychiatrist believed that Mary might be depressed.

4. What behaviors demonstrated by Mary indicate depression?

Mary was started on Elavil 25 mg QID for a trial period of six weeks.

5. Why is Elavil the tricyclic of choice for Mary? Why is Mary not a good candidate for an MAO Inhibitor? What target behaviors indicate a positive response to Elavil? What side effects of Elavil should the nursing staff be especially alert for?

Four months later, Mary's pacing ceased. She gained 3 pounds; she slept most of the night at long intervals. She responded positively to verbal commands. Her cognitive ability returned to her previous level of functioning. She regularly assisted the nursing staff with meals, cleaning the tables and stacking trays. Mary smiled regularly and looked forward to her daughter's visits. Her daughter talked to the nursing staff about the possibility of bringing Mary home again, since she was now working only part-time.

6. Outline a discharge plan for Mary. Include community resources that provide support and preventive services. Be specific and consider the environment to which Mary will return. What educational outcomes are indicated for Mary's family?

❑

At Broome Community College, NY, Wendy Heckman has developed two pointed "scenarios" as she calls them, which students receive at the beginning of a fourth-semester nursing home clinical. They become part of a post-conference, and students explore Heckman's written questions and others by role-playing the characters in the scenarios. In the questions Heckman poses, as in the open-ended questions she poses, it is clear that for her, as for teachers everywhere, the teaching of gerontological nursing includes learning activities which prompt students to reflect on the meanings they bring to caring for the elderly.

Scenario One

Tom Katt is a 65 year old gentleman admitted to your unit from the ACF early this afternoon. His medical diagnoses are multi-infarct dementia and osteoarthritis. He is ambulatory with a cane. He is hard-of-hearing, wears glasses, and has upper and lower dentures which do not fit well. Medications include inderal and naprosyn.

1. How will you orient him to his new environment?
2. What assessments can you make?

3. Tom has a catastrophic reaction. How does this manifest itself? Why did it happen? How might it have been avoided? How can we 'handle' this reaction?
4. You begin to notice day/night reversal. What could be done to modify Tom's distress?
5. The clinical assistant informs you that Tom's appetite has been poor for the past few days. He has been unusually quiet and somnolent. What might this mean? What assessments will you make?

Scenario Two

Jane Doe is a 75 year old new admission to your unit. She has right hemiparesis, hypertension, diabetes, and bilateral cataracts. She lived at home with her spouse, John, in a high-rise handicapped-accessible apartment until her CVA. Her intent is to return home following rehabilitation.

Jane is fiercely independent. She is easily frustrated by the limits placed on her by staff, as well as by her functional deficits. She is frequently sarcastic and demanding. John is devoted; he visits twice daily for long intervals of time.

Delores is Jane's clinical assistant. Delores has been a resident assistant for 25 years. She is rigid and impersonal. The other clinical assistants complain about her 'roughness,' but look to her as a spokesperson for the group.

Susie is the unit's team leader. She graduated one year ago. She calls the residents 'Honey.' She defers to Delores.

You are the Nursing Supervisor. Jane has complained to you that Delores ignores her, and makes her wait an exorbitant length of time to be assisted with ADLs. She demands you change assignments.

1. What assessments can you make about Jane, Delores, and Susie. Consider Erikson, Maslow, supports, defense mechanisms, coping strategies, loss, etc.
2. Who is the real leader?
3. How might you respond?

Jane makes progress with her therapy, and is now permitted to transfer herself independently during the 7:00 am to 9:00 pm hours. Jane transfers herself at 9:30 pm tonight because her call bell has gone unanswered. She falls, fracturing her femur. Jane is hospitalized for 6 weeks (complications of pneumonia and urosepsis developed postoperatively). Upon her return to the facility, you notice that Jane appears frail, withdrawn, and passive. She has a stage 3 decubitus on her coccyx and has multiple skin tears. She is wearing an incontinent brief.

    4. What assessments have you made? What effects have stress and change had on Jane? How will you work with Jane to promote health and restore independence?

    5. HOW DOES THIS SCENARIO MAKE YOU FEEL?

Open-End Questions about the Clinical Experience

The essence of nursing is—

Old people are—

A nursing home is—

People who work in Long-term Care—

This rotation will be/was—

❑

As a final learning activity in this section, we offer as examples of still another approach a seminar format developed at Community College of Philadelphia, PA, for which students must prepare by watching a video located in the nursing lab and reading specific articles. Both seminars address central gerontologic nursing problems.

COMMUNITY COLLEGE OF PHILADELPHIA
DEPARTMENT OF NURSING
Seminar: Adaption to Chronic Illness

At the end of this seminar, the student will:
1. Discuss the three stage process of family caregivers coping with dementia.
2. Identify altered family process in the families of clients with chronic illness.
3. Assess the hardiness characteristic in clients.

Assignment:
—View *My Mother, My Father*
—Read:
- Pollack, 1999 Response to Chronic Illness: Analysis of Psychological and Physiological Adaptation. (Summary attached)
- Wilson, 1989, Family Caregiving For A Relative With Alzheimer Dementia: Coping With Negative Choices. (Summary attached)

Discussion Questions:
1. How did the families in the film evidence behaviors consistent with the stages of taking it on, going through it, and turning it over? Be specific.
2. What nursing interventions are most helpful to families during each stage?
3. How did the families in the film demonstrate hardiness? Give specific examples.

* See Chapter 4

Responses to Chronic Illness:
The Hardiness Characteristic*

Hardiness characteristic is a specific set of attitudes toward challenge, commitment and control that mediate the stress response. Adaptation to chronic illness is similar regardless of diagnosis.

Hardy people are:

- More likely to engage in health-related activities related to physiologic adaptation.

- More likely to participate in patient education programs specific to their diagnosis.

- Able to tolerate life changes and stresses.

---

* Pollock, S. Duffy, M.E.: The Health-Related Hardiness Scale: Development and Psychometric Analysis. Nursing Research 39 (4), 218-222.

Hardiness is seen as a personality resource that buffers the negative effects of stress. People can remain healthy under stress but may also benefit if they see the stress as opportunities for mastery and personal growth.

Hardiness is believed to have three components: control, commitment and challenge.

Control—action to promote health and response to stress.

Definition:
Sense of mastery or self-confidence needed to appropriately appraise and interpret health stressors.

Measurement:
Presence of health locus of control appropriate for health stressor.

Commitment—strong sense of commitment to self and own health.

Definition:
Motivation and competence to effectively cope with the threat of a health stressor.

Measurement:
Presence of active involvement in efforts to maintain or improve health.

Challenge—see change as stimuli rather than threat.

Definition:
Reappraisal of health stressor as stimulating and potentially beneficial; an opportunity for growth.

Measurement:
Presence of flexibility, and persistence in coping with health stressors.

These are things a hardy person might say:

I am in control of my health.
I can be as healthy as I want to be.
If I take the right actions, I can stay healthy.
I take care of myself.
My behavior determines when I will get well.

You can also encourage hardiness by saying similar things to patients. For example, "If you take the right actions, you can stay healthy."

Pollock, S.E. Christian, B.J., Sands, D.: Responses to Chronic Illness: Analysis of Psychological and Physiological Adaptation. Nursing Research, 39 (5), 300 304.

Family Adjustment to Caring For a Member With Dementia

(adapted from Wilson, H.S. (1989). Family Caregiving for a Relative with Alzheimer's Dementia: Coping with Negative Choices. Nursing Research, 38,*2, 94-98.)*

Taking it on

Continue prior responsibilities while assuming new responsibilities—leads to major changes in lifestyle with decreased social and leisure time.

Caregiver may feel trapped and worry about the future.

Coping—self dialogue, seeking spiritual solace, unburdening with others who are experiencing the same thing.

Going Through It

Family disruptions and conflicting role demands occur; gradually, household schedules, routines, vacations are disrupted.

Caregivers feel their own life is suspended, on hold, while they devote their time, energy, and money to caring for the family member with dementia; caregiver recognizes the situation places him at personal risk.

Coping—eliminate situations which create problems; take care of family member's legal, financial, medical needs; try to set aside time to replenish self; try to access community resources; talking no longer helpful, need concrete help.

Turning It Over

After thinking about and evaluating the situation, family may decide to institutionalize client; reasons for choice vary and are complex; caregiver recognizes negative consequences of caregiving on own life.

Coping—continue to take care of legal, financial, medical needs.

COMMUNITY COLLEGE OF PHILADELPHIA
DEPARTMENT OF NURSING
Seminar: Aging—Dealing with the Losses

This seminar and simulation exercise occur in the second year of study, after the students have participated in the well-elder experience and have explored a health maintenance focus for older adults. With the perspective gained from these learning activities, students are able to discuss the losses of aging in a broader context.

Objective 1:   List common losses the older adult experiences.

Objective 2:   Describe the meaning to the older adult of the losses.

Methodology: Simulation Exercise

Tell the students to come to seminar with three pieces of paper. On each piece of paper, the student will write down the three most significant possessions they now have. The possessions can be material items, i.e., T.V., or it can be a concept, i.e., independence, daily contact with family, or ability to control life. Tell the students to form small groups of 6 to 8 people and go around the small group and give up one possession first, and then around the group again and give up a second possession. This is to simulate the multiple losses encountered by the older adult. Allow the groups some time to discuss the meaning of the losses to them and why they chose to keep the third possession as the most significant. Identify common behavioral responses to loss.

Objective 3:   Identify nursing measures which can be used in dealing with physical and behavioral changes resulting from losses.
Methodology:

a) View the film: *My Mother, My Father** or selected vignettes from *Dad** or *The Sunshine Boys** [see Chapter 4]. Ask the students to identify the types of losses experienced by the older adults in the film.

b) Ask the students to interview a resident in the nursing home and discuss the resident's perception of relocation to the nursing home. What does the resident miss most? What significant changes have occurred in the resident's life? Identify behavioral responses to loss, i.e., fear, anxiety, hopelessness, guilt, helplessness, acceptance.

c) Discussion of Nursing Measures

1. Utilize communication skills to determine the meaning of the losses to the older adult, and to identify factors that influence the impact of possession loss, i.e., culture, spiritual beliefs, socio-economic status.
2. Allow time for the older person to express feelings and concerns about the losses.
3. Make a special effort to allow the older adult to retain some important possessions when moving to the nursing home.
4. Encourage reminiscence about previous life-styles and losses (i.e., 2 women in film who are talking about 43rd St.).
5. Provide opportunity for older adults to shift interests in order to substitute for losses, i.e., woman in film who started a rhythm band; woman in film who started physical therapy classes.
6. Focus attention on client strengths and effective coping mechanisms.
7. Assist the client through the stages of adaptive grieving, recognizing that the process may be prolonged, perhaps 6-12 months.

❑

Learning Experiences
for Developing Ethical Reasoning and Sensitivity

Gail Cobe, Ohlone College, CA, has, since the early days of the project, been engaged in a wide range of activities addressing ethical issues and problems that arise in care of the elderly. She prepared the following set of learning experiences, which have been used both with students and with faculty and nurses, and an annotated bibliography on gerontological nursing and ethics that follows the set of learning activities.

LEARNING EXPERIENCES
FOR DEVELOPING ETHICAL REASONING AND
SENSITIVITY TO DIVERSITY

Gail Cobe, MSN RN
Ohlone College

Exercise 1

*The following exercise is a modified version of one from **Values and ethics for a caring staff in nursing homes** by Kris Urv-Wong MHA and Rosalie Kane, DSW.*

The goal of the exercise is to help students identify their own values and better understand those family, social class, historical era, and cultural influences which helped to shape them. This exercise helps students internalize their knowledge that personal values differ from person to person.

Exercise

Talk to two elders and ask them about the world events that occurred when they were growing up. Ask them how those events affected their lives. Imagine now that you had lived through a similar event. Would it change the way you think about life or change your personal values?

Talk to one elder who has a different cultural background from yours. Ask what is important in his or her life and about values that person holds. Which values are similar to yours? Which are different?

Talk to another student who has a different cultural background than yours. Ask what is important in his or her life and what types of values affect that person's learning and nursing. Which values are similar to yours? Which are different?

Questions for Discussion
1. Do you think values change over time?
2. Do you think that your values differ from the values held by other students or those held by those persons you provide with nursing care?

Exercise 2

*The following exercise is also modified from an exercise in **Values and ethics for a caring staff in nursing homes** by Kris Urv-Wong MHA and Rosalie Kane, DSW. Students learn that having the right to make choices and to be able to act upon the choices or to have a surrogate act upon them is an important freedom called autonomy.*

Exercise

Give the students 10 minutes to list all of the choices they make in a typical day.

Choices made at school, at home, and on the job should be included.

Discuss

1. Have the students identify which choices are most important to them and discuss what makes them important.

Exercise

Ask the students to cross out the three choices they would be willing to give up each day. Ask them then to circle the three choices they would not be willing to give up.

Discuss

1. Have the students discuss the choices they crossed out and why they were willing to give them up.
2. Have them discuss the choices they circled and why they would not give them up.

Exercise

Have the students make a list of all of the choices a nursing home resident makes during a typical day and compare it with their list.

Discuss

How many of the choices are the same? Does the amount of choices differ? Ask the students if they believe it is important to have choices. Does the importance of choice change if a person is elderly, if a person is in a nursing home or if a person is cognitively impaired (having a dementia like Alzheimers)?

Exercise 3

*This exercise is adapted from an exercise in **Module 2** in **Enhancing autonomy in long term care: A training manual for nursing homes** by Dr. Debra David and Dr. Martha Pelaez. This exercise also focuses on helping the students recognize that although people may share the same values, they often choose different actions to express those values. The discussion which follows the exercise helps students learn to listen to others and views of the world.*

This scenario describes an imaginary situation. As you read it, think of yourself in that situation. Then answer the three questions at the end.

Exercise

You are a 78-year-old resident living in a nursing facility because of a diabetes-related amputation of one foot, low vision, and moderately severe arthritis. You are wheelchair-bound. You can usually move your own chair (unless your arthritis is bothering you a lot), but you need assistance to transfer to the toilet, get in and out of bed, bathe, and dress.

You entered the home as a private patient almost three years ago after your amputation, but you've been on Medicaid for over a year. The home is one of the better ones in your community. Many staff members have worked there a long time, care about the residents, and are usually fairly responsive to your requests for help (though you've had a few urinary accidents in evening because of slow responses to your call for help with toileting). Many residents, including your roommate, are confused. However, you have two friends among the alert residents with whom you get along well. You participate in most activities, though you find them boring because they are designed mainly for less alert residents. You are fortunate to have brought your own TV. Also, you have your own phone (which your daughter's family has paid for since you became eligible for Medicaid).

Your daughter, son-in-law, and three grandchildren (in late teens and early twenties) live in town. Your daughter visits at least once a week, often with another family member. Once or twice a month she brings you to their house for dinner or takes you out. Your son and his wife live several hours away; they usually visit every two months. Sometimes friends from the church you used to attend or the neighborhood you used to live in come to visit.

You have developed a heart irregularity that your doctor thinks is likely to cause you to die suddenly. While it's hard to predict when that would happen, the doctor's best guess is that you would live no more than a year. It could be easily corrected with a pacemaker, which the doctor strongly recommends. Inserting a pacemaker is routine and low-risk. It is done with local anesthesia. With the pacemaker, you could live many more years. Your vision and arthritis are likely to worsen slowly.

1. Would you want to have the pacemaker inserted?

   ❏ YES   ❏ NO

2. How sure are you that your choice is the best one for you?

   ❏ Very sure   ❏ Somewhat sure   ❏ Unsure

3. How important were each of the following factors in making this decision?

	Extremely important	Somewhat important	Not important at all
• Letting nature take its course.	3	2	1
• Preserving my quality of life.	3	2	1
• Living as long as possible.	3	2	1
• Being able to make my own decisions.	3	2	1
• Considering the amount of burden I would be to others.	3	2	1
• Having privacy.	3	2	1
• Being comfortable and as pain free as possible.	3	2	1
• Being able to relate to family and friends.	3	2	1
• Considering my level of physical restriction.	3	2	1
• Being able to die in a short while rather than linger on.	3	2	1
• Recognizing that my life is sacred, no matter what its quality.	3	2	1
• Being as independent as possible.	3	2	1
• Considering the cost involved to Medicaid for my care.	3	2	1
• Considering the opportunity to participate in meaningful activities.	3	2	1
• Other factors (specify):	3	2	1
	3	2	1

Discussion

1. What decision did each person make? What were the main reasons for each decision?
2. If a patient you were caring for were to make a different decision than yours, how would you feel?
3. If a patient in a similar situation were to refuse the pacemaker, how should professional staff respond?

Exercise 4

The use of the following modified exercise, from Dr. Debra David and Dr. Martha Pelaez's training manual, helps students learn the ethical importance and clinical relevancy to facilitating resident or patient participation in care planning. Students are encouraged through the role play to act as advocates, empower residents, and use the art of persuasion. They practice therapeutic communication and the art of negotiation, and have the opportunity to view a situation from the vantage point of other disciplines.

Exercise

Have students break up into small groups to do the role play. Give them 15 minutes.

Role Play: The Right to Fall?

THE PARTS:

> 1. Mrs. L., the resident
> 2. Mrs. M., the nurse
> 3. Miss N., the social worker
>   *If your group has four members-*
> 4. Mrs. P., the physical therapist

THE SITUATION:

Mrs. L. is very unsteady on her feet because of Parkinson's disease. Based on an evaluation, the physical therapist has recommended a walker. The therapist fitted her with a walker and taught her how to use it. However, Mrs. L. refuses. She sometimes uses a cane and sometimes walks without it.

Mrs. L. has fallen three times in the past two weeks, twice when using the cane and once when walking without it. None of the falls has caused more than minor bruises. On one of the falls, Mrs. L. landed on the foot of another resident and almost knocked her down. Staff members are concerned that she will injure herself or another resident more seriously.

ACTION:

You are meeting to discuss the situation and negotiate a solution that will be acceptable to everyone.

INSTRUCTIONS TO PLAYERS:

Mrs. L.: You do not want to use the walker. In your view, it means "giving up." It's important to you to be independent and mobile. The walker is very slow and awkward, especially in the crowded hallways. Although you know that you are likely to fall again, you'd rather take the risk of some bumps and bruises.

Mrs. M.: You feel strongly that Mrs. L. should use the walker because of the risk of major injury to herself and/or other residents. You think that Mrs. L. does not realize how serious a hip fracture or other injury could be. Also, you are concerned that surveyors will cite your facility for poor care if someone is injured.

Miss N.: You have mixed feelings about this situation. On the one hand, you appreciate Mrs. L.'s desire to be independent and her right to decide for herself. On the other hand, you are aware of the real risk of injury. Also, you think that Mrs. L.'s family may sue if she is seriously hurt. Her daughter has been upset about the falls and wants her mother to be protected.

Mrs. P.: You agree with Mrs. M. that the walker is necessary. You feel that Mrs. L. should get used to it now, before her condition gets worse.

Discussion

Ask each group to share their experience. Did members feel that their views were heard? Were members able to identify communication techniques which were nontherapeutic. What communication techniques were effective? Ask the group to identify the ethical principles which surfaced as a result of the role play. Was the group able to reach consensus about a plan?

Exercise 5

Informed consent is a hallmark for autonomous decision making and is required for all health care decisions and yet the provision of information may come into conflict with respecting an individual's and his/her family's culture and preferences. This scenario, modified from Dr. Debra David and Dr. Martha Pelaez's training manual, helps the students think through this dilemma and recognize that there are some persons who prefer not to know about their condition and have the right to refuse informativeness.

Mr. Yamamoto:

Mr. Yamamoto, age 83, was recently admitted to Oak Manor Convalescent Hospital to recuperate after an operation to remove a cancerous spleen. A recent check-up, however, showed that the cancer had spread. The doctor believes that further treatment would be futile and that the cancer is terminal.

His two daughters ask the nursing home staff not to tell Mr. Yamamoto about the prognosis but to continue to make him as comfortable as possible. They explain that in Japanese culture, it is not customary to inform patients when their conditions are terminal. Mr. Yamamoto came to the United States from Japan with his parents when he was 15; he speaks good English and appears to be "Americanized." He has asked the day charge nurse to tell him when he will be able to go home.

1. What should the day charge nurse tell Mr. Yamamoto?
2. Mr. Yamamoto has not directly asked for information about his medical condition. How can the staff in the nursing home determine whether Mr. Yamamoto really wants full information about his medical condition?
3. Should the possibility of a "do not resuscitate" (DNR) order be discussed with Mr. Yamamoto and/or his daughters? Why or why not?

Annotated Bibliography, Ethical Reasoning
Gail Cobe, MSN, RN

A.A.R.P. Ethics Committees (1991) Allies in long term care (VHS Video). Washington, D.C., American Association of Retired Persons.

This 30 minute video and presenter guide is made available with twenty-five copies of guide book for twenty dollars. The video encourages ethical reasoning on the topics of refusal to accept treatment, restraints and freedom, and the right to refuse to eat. A simulated ethics committee demonstrates ethical deliberation.

Collopy, Bart J. (1988). Autonomy in long term care: Some crucial distinctions. The *Gerontologist*. 28. 10-17.

Discusses the principle of autonomy as a broad concept. Emphasis is on maintaining autonomy for the frail elderly even when their ability to execute an activity, becomes limited or dependent on others. It explores competent and incapacitated decision making and its eight cases can easily be used for classroom discussion.

Committee on Ethics Guidelines on Withdrawing or Withholding Food and Fluid (1987) American Nurses Association, Kansas City, Missouri.

These guidelines focus upon the circumstances under which it is morally permissible to withhold food and fluid. This is a must for all nursing students and practitioners

Cranford, R. E. (1988) The persistent vegetative state: The medical reality (Getting the Facts Straight). *Hastings Center Report. February/ March. 18(1) 27-32.*

As the author states, "the first step in any bioethical dilemma is to collect the facts and to understand the medical reality of the situation". This article succinctly differentiates brain death from persistent vegetative state and describes the clinical picture, prognosis and landmark legal cases associated with each.

David, D. & Pelaez, M. (1992). Enhancing autonomy in long term care: A training manual for nursing homes. San Jose Gerontology & Education Center, San Jose State University.

This training manual is comprised of five modules intended to help caregivers understand the complex concept of autonomy as it relates to competing values in the long-term care settings. Case studies and other experiential methods are used to help students develop skills in solving ethical dilemmas. The following topics are covered: informing elders, understanding elder's values and preferences, assessing decision-making capacity, negotiating care plans, helping elders with impaired decision-making capacity, and promoting meaningful choice. Lesson plans are pragmatic, learning exercises, overheads and handouts are provided, and evaluation tools are included. A great asset for any educational institution and one which helps students learn to think critically about ethics.

Hofland, B. F. (Ed.). (1988) Autonomy and long term care. [Supplementary Issue]. *The Gerontologist, 28.*

The content of this supplemental issue includes articles from participants in the Retirement Research Foundation's Initiative on Personal Autonomy in Long Term Care. Articles focus on the meaning of autonomy, empowerment possibilities for the elderly, decision making, guardianship, informed consent, etc. It is a thought provoking issue and one which would be of interest to nursing home clinicians and educators concerned with teaching students about the psychosocial domain of their practice.

Kane, R. A. & Caplan, A. L. (1990). *Everyday Ethics: Resolving Dilemmas in Nursing Home Life.* New York: Springer.

This book can be read in its entirety or in parts. It describes the way things are in a nursing home and the role the nursing home plays in society. The heart of the book are cases which ring true to all who live and work in a long-term care facility. Some ethical dilemmas which are explored include restraints, the demanding resident, handling the death of a resident, and managing roommates. Commentaries on the cases by various experts in the field are provided. This is an excellent source of information for faculty and one which provides cases and ideas on how to discuss same in an ethical framework.

Kayser-Jones, J., Dans, A., Wiener, C., & Higgins, S. (1989). An ethical analysis of an elders treatment. *Nursing Outlook. 37* (6). 267-270.

The course of medical treatment, nursing care, and death of Mrs. M., an 85 year old woman with Alzheimer's Disease, is examined from the perspectives of non-maleficence, the ANA code for nurses, and the ethic of caring. A worthwhile reading and trigger for discussion on aging and nursing ethics.

Keatings, M. & Dick, D. (1989). Ethics and politics of resource allocation: The role of nursing. *Journal of Business Ethics, 8.187-192.*

Although this article was written by two Canadian nurses, the major social and policy issues they discuss are those that face American nurses as well. Issues discussed include allocation of resources; who gets what and how, i.e., use of nursing personnel, fragmentation of care, and time constraints in meeting patient needs. The authors call for nurses to empower themselves and to be more actively involved in policy analysis and development, and to expand their contribution to society. An interesting article for an issues class.

Lidz, Charles, & Arnold, R.M. (1990). Institution constraints on autonomy. *Generations, supplement 65-68.*

This article is an interesting social analysis which describes the structure of long-term care and its effects in reducing autonomy. It compares the nursing home with Erving Goffman's notion of "total institution." Students should read it during a nursing home clinical and discuss how the home inhibits autonomy. Then they can make recommendations which restructure the home and promote autonomy.

Post, S. G. (1990). Nutrition, hydration and the demented elderly. *The Journal of Medical Humanities. 11 (4) 18-191.*

The author argues against providing artificial nutrition and hydration. He states these interventions can cause harm and in many cases are futile procedures which should be avoided. It is his contention that health practitioners are uncomfortable with withholding and withdrawing nutrition and hydration and view them as euthanasia. A good article to trigger a discussion on an important and emotionally charged topic.

Printz, L. A. (1988). Is withholding hydration a valid comfort measure in the terminally ill? *Geriatrics, 43 (11) 84-88.*

The author suggests that dehydration is an analgesic and therefore withholding hydration from a dying patient may be a comfort measure and ethically correct. Suggestions are given for supportive measures. Staffs' emotional reactions are explored.

Rouse, Fenella (1988). Linng wills in the long term care facility. *The Journal of Long Term Care Administration* (Summer) 1419.

The answers to questions about who decides about life sustaining medical treatment, determining capacity, and advance directives are addressed. This article can be used to help students understand the issues health facilities face.

Thobaben, M. (1992). Whose life is it anyway? *Journal of Holistic Nursing, 10* (3) 2 250.

This article identifies the dilemma experienced by nurses when there are questions as to what treatment is acceptable to the patient and under what conditions. Although this situation arises in the ICU it elucidates the nurse's moral responsibility as educator and patient advocate.

Urv-Wong, Kris & Kane, R. (1991). Values and Ethics for a caring staff in nursing homes: A training guide. The University of Minnesota Long-Term Care Decisions Resource Center, Minneapolis, Minnesota.

Although the curriculum for this guide was designed for nursing assistants who work in the aging network, many of the exercises can easily be adapted for nursing students. There are ten 1 1/2 hour classes. Classes focus on defining ethical concepts such as autonomy, beneficence, justice, death and dying, and decision making.

Wurzbach, M. E. (1990). The dilemma of withholding or withdrawing nutrition. *Image (22)* 4 226-229.

This article explores the debate regarding withholding and withdrawing nutrition in persons of all ages. The right to life, dying with dignity, burdens of treatment as well as legal considerations are discussed. It is concise, well written, easy to read and an important source of knowledge if nurses are going to make decisions using moral knowledge.

---

[8] Palmore, E.B., (1986). *The facts on aging quiz.* New York: Springer Publishing Company, Inc.

[9] National Institute on Aging. *What is your aging IQ?* Bethesda: U.S. Department of Health and Human Services, U.S. Public Health Service.

[10] Waters, V. (Ed.). (1991). *Teaching gerontology.* New York: National League for Nursing Press. 126–128.

[11] Farrell, Jane. (1990). In *Nursing care of the older person.* (p. 22). Philadelphia: J.B. Lippincott & Co.

[12] Waters, V. (Ed.) (1991). *Teaching gerontology* (pp. 96–105). New York: National League for Nursing Press.

[13] Longfellow, H. W. (1891). *The complete poetical works of Henry Wadsworth Longfellow.* (p. 313) New York: Houghton Mifflin & Co.

[14] "Who will hug the elderly?" by Patricia Conger Walsh, R.N. is reprinted with permission of *The Nursing Spectrum.* Greater Philadelphia/Tri-State Edition, Vol. 2, No. 2, November 30, 1992, p. 5 (Originally published in the Greater New York/New Jersey Metro Edition).

[15] Remnet, V. L. (1989). *Understanding older adults: An experiential approach to learning.* Lexington, MA: D.C. Heath & Company.

[16] Tagliareni, E., Sherman, S., Waters, V. & Mengel, A. (1991). Participatory clinical education: Reconceptualizing the clinical learning environment. *Nursing & Health Care, 12, 248–263.*

[17] Bellanca, J. Fogarty, R. (1991). *Blueprints for thinking in the cooperative classroom.* (pp. 49, 291). Palatine, IL: Skylight Publishing, Inc.

Chapter 3

Annotated Print Resources

We include periodical articles and textbooks on the topic of gerontological nursing. The list of articles is selective; only articles that faculty in the Community College-Nursing Home Partnership project have used regularly and find particularly useful are included.

Articles

Breakey, B. (1990). What is a geriatric nurse? *Geriatric Nursing. 11*, 11.

A poetic view of a day in the life of a geriatric nurse—"some really special kind of nurse." A must for students at all levels, to engender appreciation of their nursing colleagues in long-term care.

Burke, A., Shirley, E., Baker, C., Deno, L. & Tagliareni, E. (1990). Perceptions from the nursing home: How we can make a difference. *Imprint, 37*, 62-65.

Nursing students tell stories about their unique experiences in the nursing home. These experiences helped to transform the students into effective and competent caregivers and to change their perceptions about the role of the registered nurse in long-term care. Can serve as "testimonials" for students embarking on a nursing home clinical experience. May also be used to assist in convincing faculty and nursing home personnel of the value of the nursing home clinical.

Hahn, Aloyse. (1970). It's tough to be old. *American Journal of Nursing,* August, 85-88

Written in the first person, this article describes the feelings and concerns of a nursing home resident. It explains behaviors students observe, and can be a catalyst for discussions about understanding the special needs of older adults in the nursing home. Use early in nursing home clinical; good post-conference topic in weeks 1 or 2.

Kutschke, M. (1988). Only for the moment. *Geriatric Nursing* Sept/Oct, 296-297

The author describes her work (as a student) with a 94 year old, anxious, cognitively compromised woman. She initiated a plan of active nursing interventions expecting success in allaying the resident's anxiety and modifying behaviors. This short, insightful article helps students gain a *care* (as opposed to cure) perspective as they follow the author to her conclusion that she was able to bring comfort to the resident "only for the moment."

Lewis, K. (1986). What it takes to be a preceptor. *Canadian Nurse,* 82(12), 18-19.

A brief overview of the qualities desirable in a preceptor for students. Reveals that the experience is both challenging and rewarding. "Must" reading for both preceptors and students.

Qualey, T. (1989). Antigone admits her father to a nursing home. *American Journal of* Nursing, 89(11), 1470-1472

A conscientious daughter (Antigone) struggles with the decision to have her father (Oedipus) admitted to a nursing home in this fictional melodrama. Supports the concept that the nursing home CAN be the best place for the care of an older adult. A light-hearted look at the struggles many families encounter. Useful for students preparing for a nursing home clinical experience.

Rader, J., Doan, J. & Schwab, M. (1985). How to decrease wandering: a form of agenda behavior. *Geriatric Nursing* (4), 196-199.

A classic article describing interventions that nurses can use to deal with wandering, confusion, and aggression in the nursing home resident. Rader et al hypothesize that these behaviors stem from feelings of loneliness and separation, and they recommend tested actions and communication techniques to help the resident feel connected and secure. Students find this article extremely helpful; it deals with issues they encounter daily in a nursing home rotation, and presents case studies which are clear and compelling.

Rice, L. (1991). Do we discriminate against the elderly? *Nursing 88, 18*(3), 44-45.

Examines the negative view of old age held by many in the United States. Cites research on nurses' attitudes and notes that education and self-awareness can assist in ridding our profession of bias against the elderly. Useful as a consciousness raising tool for students, faculty, and staff—especially acute care nurses.

Tellis-Nayak, V. (1989). Nurses aides and their burden of two cultures. In *Successful nurse aid management in nursing homes* by J. Day & H. Berman, Phoenix: Oryx Press. 5-13.

Four case studies describe the personal world of the nurse aide, a world far removed from the middle-class culture of the modern nursing home. The author speaks highly of these committed, responsible, yet under paid caregivers, and suggests that successful nursing homes are those that create an institutional culture that nurtures the aide and fosters a family spirit to evoke loyalty and devotion. Students should read this article as a basis for discussing how to establish collaborative relationships with nursing assistants as they learn management of nursing care in the nursing home.

Wilson, H. (1989). Family caregiving for a relative with Alzheimer's dementia: Coping with negative choices. *Nursing Research, 38*(2), 94-98.

Describes the process of family caregiving as a three-stage phenomenon: (1) taking it on, (2) going through it, and (3) turning it over. Each stage has characteristics, problems, and coping strategies for dealing with a series of negative choices. Useful in a second level seminar together with the film, *My Mother, My Father* (see Chapter 4). Students relate findings in the research article to the caregivers in the films, and discuss nursing interventions for each stage to ease the caregiver burden.

Textbooks

Gloria Kuhlman, Ohlone College, CA reviewed all major textbooks in the field of gerontological nursing, and prepared annotations.

Annotated Bibliography, Gerontology Textbooks
by Gloria Kuhlman, DNS, RN Ohlone College

This annotated bibliography contains texts that may be used by students in a geriatric nursing course and books that may be used by the faculty as resources to enhance the course content.

Birchenall, J. M. & Streight, M. E. (1993). *Care of the older adult* (3rd Ed.). Philadelphia: J.B. Lippincott Co.

This text has an emphasis on preventative and restorative nursing. The text does not provide a basic overview of anatomy and physiology or nutrition, but has study questions at the end of each chapter that relate medical/surgical or psychiatric issues to the topic. The first eight chapters describe the aging population, elder developmental tasks, elder community needs, the aging process, drug therapy, and activities of daily living. The final chapters focus on restorative care with nursing care plans, adaptations for home care, and support groups for the caregiver. Each chapter has a system focus with several diseases as models.

Burke, M. M, & Walsh, M. B. (1992). *Gerontologic nursing—Care of the frail elderly*. St. Louis: Mosby Year Book.

This text is designed to be a comprehensive text for all levels of nursing. The focus on the frail elder (over 75) limits the scope of the book. The authors acknowledge the lack of information on this group of elders, but emphasize the extreme need for information related to the care of the multiple health problems of this vulnerable population. The book progresses from a general introduction to gerontologic nursing to a focus on the unique health care needs of the frail elder person. The chapters select a complex functional issue and provide age related changes in the elder, commonly observed pathology, and the nursing care. The specific caregiving techniques are provided for acute care, nursing homes, and home care. There are diagrams and illustrations that help enhance the content discussion.

Ebersole, P. & Hess, P. (1990). *Toward healthy aging: Human needs and nursing response.* (3rd Ed.) St. Louis: The C.V. Mosby Co.

This comprehensive text provides a detailed discussion of gerontic nursing, and therefore focuses on all aspects of the elder from wellness to illness rather than just an illness or scientific principles focus. This larger focus is useful to students in longer semester courses, but may prove unmanageable in a short course approach. The text is divided into three sections. The first section focuses on aging theories, health and wellness, wellness assessments including laboratory findings, and chronic wellness problems. The second section has five units that focus on the hierarchy of needs for the older person. The first unit (biologic needs) provides information on basic needs and assessments. It includes a chapter on drug use and abuse as well as several appendices related to drug use in the elderly. The second unit focuses on safety and security as it relates to mobility, personal security, environmental needs, economic and legal considerations, and the frail elder. This unit also provides home, community, and elder abuse assessment information. The third unit focuses on belonging. The issues of sexuality, relationship networks, and social isolation are covered. The fourth unit focuses on self-esteem and self-respect. This unit covers role transitions, role crises, mental health issues, and cultural differences in the elderly population. The fifth unit, self-actualization, looks at the aging as a "peak experience." The focus is on learning and growing as well as transcending into death. The final section of the text focuses on the nurse: the development of gerontic nursing, nursing roles in the institution and community, ethics of caring, and a chapter that provides the perspectives of gerontic nurse pioneers. This text may prove to be difficult (length and reading level) for the undergraduate student, but for graduate students or faculty resource material it is excellent.

Eliopoulos, C. (1993) *Gerontological nursing* (3rd Ed.) Philadelphia: J.B. Lippincott Co.

This text is a basic introduction to the nursing care of the elderly. The book is divided into four units which include: understanding the aging population, promoting wellness and self-care, pathologies of aging, and gerontological care issues. The first unit provides basic facts on aging, family issues, common changes in aging, and a chapter on ethnic elders. Each chapter in the second unit promotes wellness and assessments for well elders. In the third unit, the individual systems are covered by providing assessments via review of related disorders and via appropriate nursing interventions. This section also contains a well written chapter on geriatric pharmacology that includes pharmacokinetics in the elderly and a chapter on geriatric rehabilitation. The final unit provides separate chapters on legal and ethical considerations of the elderly population as well as chapters on elder services and gerontological nursing in diverse care settings.

Miller, C. A. (1990). *Nursing care of older adults: Theory and practice.* Glenview, Illinois: Scott, Foresman/Little, Brown Higher Education.

This text provides an organized overview of geriatric care. The chapters are grouped into five sections which include: an introduction to care, changes in psychosocial functioning, changes in physiological functioning, changes related to comfort and pleasure, and multidimensional aspects of care. Each chapter provides age-related changes, risk factors, functional consequences, assessments, interventions, and educational resources related to the system covered. Charts and illustrations provide emphasis to the important points by providing an overview of the chapter's content.

Staab, A. S. & Lyles, M. F. (1990). *Manual of geriatric nursing.* Glenview, Illinois: Scott, Foresman/Little Brown Higher Education.

This manual provides information to help the nurse provide care for the older adult in a variety of clinical settings. The manual emphasizes disorders most common in the elderly with management of the disorder presented in outline form for easy reading. There is an emphasis on total care of the older adult with sections on social, psychological, and financial aspects of the care. A variety of caregiving settings are covered from acute to home care. The first two sections of the manual provide information on broad health issues, while the third (and longest) provides management of specific disease processes utilizing the outline format.

Wold, G. (1993). *Basic geriatric nursing*. St. Louis: Mosby.

This basic text takes a gerontic nursing focus. The five part text includes an overview of aging, normal physiologic changes, the nurses role in the care of the older adult, providing care within the nursing process through the use of functional health patterns, and medications in the older adult. The chapters contain boxes and tables that are easy to read and provide the student with information related to the basic concepts of each chapter. The chapters provide a brief summary of concepts at the end of the chapter, but omit practice questions or references for further reading.

Resource Books

Baines, E. M. (1991). *Perspectives on gerontological nursing*. Newbury Park: Sage Publications.

This text is designed to provide the nurse with a resource of not only the chapter's information, but a large list of references as well. Each original chapter is written by a nurse with the focus on providing scientific evidence for the interventions described. The emphasis of this book is the need for recognition of the positive effect that nursing interventions can have on the health care of older adults. The first part of the book focuses on the promotion of healthy aging by describing the role of the nurse, describing developmental perspectives in aging, and sociological issues that affect nursing care. The second part of the book focuses on actual or potential problems of the older adult and the maintenance, treatment, and restorative nursing care provided.

Corr, D. M. & Corr, C. A. (1990). *Nursing care in an aging society*. New York: Springer Publishing Co.

This text is designed as a resource for nurses. The editors of the text indicate this may be used for students, but the reading level and complexity of the text would provide for a difficult learning experience for the beginner. The brevity of each chapter with multiple references provides the experienced nurse with a quick resource and multiple references for further reading. The text is divided into four parts. Part I provides nursing approaches to the elderly. Part II emphasizes physical needs of the elderly. Part III focuses on the psychosocial needs of elderly individuals. Part IV has an emphasis on the delivery of nursing care to an aged society. The content discussion in each chapter is enhanced by the use of multiple tables to provide information in a capsule format.

Eliopoulos, C. (1990). *Caring for the elderly in diverse care settings.* Philadelphia: J.B. Lippincott Co.

This text was designed to be a resource for nurses from multiple care settings. The overview ranges from characteristics of the older person, service needs, available services, the complexities of long-term care, and acute care needs and risks of the elderly. The text is divided into four parts: essentials of gerontological nursing and then gerontological nursing in the community, in acute care, and in long-term care. The essentials section focuses on normal to abnormal changes, nutritional needs, safe drug use, rehabilitation, legal issues, ethical issues, and the promotion of effective communication with the elderly. The other sections focus on issues related to the particular setting such as service use in the home care section, hospital-based assessment teams in acute care, and how to select a nursing home in long-term care.

Katz P. R., Kane, R. L., & Mezey, M. D. (1993). *Advances in long-term care* Volume 2. New York: Springer Publishing Co.

This volume reviews common issues confronting health care professional caring for the elder in long-term care. Each chapter focuses on a particular issue providing data on the issue with a focus on current knowledge and provides a long reference list for further reading. Common issues discussed include cardiac rehabilitation, treatment of pressure sores, problematic behavior, staffing in nursing facilities, environmental influences on falls, health promotion, and assisted living for the elderly. The final chapter focuses on information systems (use of computerization) in the long-term setting with an emphasis on how staff can use this process to gather and manage information on their residents.

Lueckenotte, A. G. (1990). *Pocket guide to gerontologic assessment.* St. Louis: The C.V. Mosby Co.

This pocket-sized text contains an overview of a nursing assessment of the older adult and guides for interviewing the older adult. The remaining text provides a system-by-system assessment. Each chapter systematically proceeds through the examination by providing pertinent examination techniques, normal age-related findings and variations of normal, and illustrations to increase understanding of the process.

Care Plan Manuals

There are many care plan manuals available for providing care. The following is a listing of several available manuals:

Eliopoulos, C. (1990). *Applying nursing diagnosis: Nursing care planning guides for long-term care* (3rd ed.). Baltimore: Williams & Wilkins.

Hogstel, M. O. (1992). *Clinical manual of gerontological nursing.* St. Louis: Mosby Year Book.

Loftis, P. A. & Glover, T. L. (1993). *Decision making in gerontologic nursing.* St. Louis: Mosby.

Maas, M., Buckwalter, K., & Hardy, M. A. (1991). *Nursing diagnoses and interventions for the elderly.* Redwood City, CA: Addison-Wesley Nursing.

Newman, D. K. & Smith D. A. J. (1991). *Geriatric care plans.* Springhouse, PA: Springhouse Corporation.

Chapter 4

Film and Video Resources for Teaching About the Care of Elders

The following recommendations on video resources and annotations were developed by Patricia Bentz and Barbara Van Droof, Shoreline College WA, Mary Ellen Simmons, Triton College, IL, Elaine Tagliareni, Community College of Philadelphia, along with her Northeast Cluster School colleagues at Berkshire Community College, MA and Delaware Technical and Community College, DE.

Acting Our Age
Video 60 minutes $350 purchase.
An in-depth look into the lives of six elderly women from diverse backgrounds. Women speak about their feelings and thoughts about growing old. Powerful, not all positive. Stimulates good discussion about student's own feelings and fears about aging
Direct Cinema Ltd. Film Arts Foundation. P.O. Box 69799, Los Angeles, CA, 90069

Alzheimer's 101: The Basics for Caregiving.
VHS Color 85 minutes (1989)
Gives clear, positive, realistic approaches to use while working with individuals in various stages of Alzheimer's. Important professional and
assistive caregiver issues are raised for discussion. Nursing students
find this a good teaching film for them to use with families or nursing
assistants. Recommend showing film in sections, followed by discussion after each section. Can be used in weekly or monthly sessions.
South Carolina Commission on Aging and South Carolina ETC, P.O.
Drawer L, Columbia, SC 29250.

And the Home of the Brave
VHS Color 17 minutes
Promotes an awareness of the trauma of admission to a nursing home
and demonstrates some of the losses residents face, such as loss of
identity, privacy, self-esteem, and independence. Relationships of residents with each other and with staff members are realistically portrayed. Can be used with students or nursing home staff to sensitize
them to the problems and feelings of residents. May also be used with
resident groups to promote discussion and perhaps problem-solving.
Tricepts Productions Film Library. P.O. Box 315, Franklin Lakes, NJ,
07417

A Nurse Like Mary
Video
Demonstrates correct and incorrect behaviors of geriatric caregivers.
Developed at Weber State college by Mary Ann Anderson as part of
the Community College-Nursing Home Partnership.
Weber State College, School of Allied Health Sciences, Department of
Nursing. Ogden, UT. 84408-3903 (801)626-6132

A Perspective of Hope: Scenes from the Teaching Nursing Home
VHS Color 28 minutes
An outcome of the Robert Wood Johnson Teaching Nursing Home
Project, this video examines the impact of student placement in nursing homes on the lives of students, faculty, staff members, residents,
and their families. Positively, but realistically, it presents the challenges and rewards of the nursing home clinical experience. Can be
used to "persuade" nursing faculty and nursing home staff of the rea-

sons why nursing students SHOULD be placed in nursing homes for clinical practice. Good preview for students about to embark on a first experience in a nursing home.

Fanlight Productions. 47 Halifax Street, Boston, MA, 02130. (617) 524-0980

Assessment of Mental Status: Mini-Mental Status Exam (Folstein)
Video $25
Describes the use of the mini-mental status exam, with demonstration by a nurse. Excellent introduction for students.

University of Minnesota, University Media Resources RARIG Center. 330 21st Ave S., Minneapolis MN, 55455.

Assessing the Elderly: Functional Assessment
Video 15 minutes $280 purchase (1990)
Demonstrates assessment of ADLs and IADLs in the older adult. Helpful in introductory assessment lab, and in post-conference to spark discussion related to ADLs of the older client. Brief running time contributes to usefulness for class discussion.

Concept Media Video. Irvine, CA (800) 233-7078

Assessing the Elderly: Mental and Socio-Economic Assessment
Video 16 minutes $280 purchase (1990)
Demonstrates a mental status exam and depression scale with a discussion of socioeconomic factors which influence function in the older adult. Useful in orienting students to a second-level nursing home experience in the nursing home where they will use standardized depression and cognitive assessment scales.

Concept Media Video. Irvine, CA (800) 233-7078

Aunt Hallie
Video 7 1/2 minutes $125 purchase
Delightful yarn about the narrator's Aunt Hallie who discovers a condom on her lawn and concludes that it has spread disease into her house. She takes elaborate measures to protect herself; all her actions make sense in light of her belief. This film is a creative ice-breaker for students in gerontology or mental health. Opens up topics ranging from hypochondria to aging to the strength and resourcefulness of older adults. Students become aware that although behavior may seem strange, it has meaning in light of the individual's perception of events.

Fanlight Productions. 47 Halifax Street, Boston, MA 02130. (617)524-0980.

Functional Assessment of the Elderly—Part II
Video 30 minutes $292 purchase (1990)

Demonstrates physical assessment of an older adult, illustrating changes in body systems while discussing associated functional changes and ADL alterations. Nursing interventions suggested. Well-presented content, excellent demonstration of a physical exam. Narrators sometimes difficult to understand. Excellent introduction for students.

American Journal of Nursing Educational Services Division. 555 West 57th Street, New York, NY 10019-2961. (800) CALL-AJN.

Grace
Video 58 minutes $400 purchase (1992)

A composite of previously released programs, *Living with Grace*, *Caregiving with Grace*, and *Glenn's Perspective on Grace*. It follows the life of Grace Kirkland, who suffers from Alzheimer's Disease, over a seven-year period, through the eyes of her husband, Glenn, who is the primary caregiver. Documents the different stages of progressive dementing illness and the challenge each stage presents to caregivers. The film not only vividly portrays the progression of a dementing disorder, but through the storyline describes the strength and endurance of Grace and Glenn's relationship. Excellent for seminar and postconference discussion during the nursing home clinical experience.

Video Press, University of Maryland at Baltimore School of Medicine. Suite 133, 100 Penn Street, Baltimore, MD 21201.

My Mother, My Father
VHS Color 33 minutes $335 (1985)

Depicts four families as they deal with the challenges and stresses of caring for an aging parent. Four situations are presented: a father who suffers from Alzheimer's and lives with his son and family; a mother maintained in her own home and an adult day care center by a daughter while nursing home placement is contemplated; two sisters who weigh nursing home placement against bringing their ill mother to live with one sister or the other; and an 87 year-old with several major physical problems whose spirit for life pervades her relationships in a multi-generation family. Through discussions with the four families, the video provides insights into the emotions, difficulties, and adjustments of caring for an aged parent. Can be used as a catalyst for discussions about supporting care-giving families in their choices. Students often comment that the people in this film cope well despite tremendous odds.

Terra Nova Films. 9848 South Winchester Avenue Chicago IL 60643 (312)881-8491

My Mother, My Father: Seven Years Later
35 minutes. $335. (1992)

Revisits the same four families who appeared in the video described above, exploring the changes that have occurred over the years. Useful in its entirety, or segments from both films can be used to follow one family if you wish to focus on a particular problem or

Terra Nova Films. 9848 South Winchester Avenue Chicago, IL 60643. (312)881-8491

Prevention and Management of Aggressive Behavior in the Elderly
VHS Color Two videotapes of 30 minutes each with accompanying handbook

Prevention and intervention techniques used with persons who lack impulse control and are, or can become, aggressive. Examples illustrate triggers for aggressive behaviors in a person with sensory deficits. Verbal, behavioral, and medical interventions are demonstrated. Emphasis is on prevention. Useful with both professional and non-professional caregivers. Raises ethical issues which spark discussion. Can be viewed together, separately, or in sections.

Good Samaritan Hospital and Medical Center. Portland, OR

Staying Alive: Wellness After 60
Video. 28 minutes

Focus on wellness, defined as positive health. Highlights tasks and role changes of later years and rebukes aging myths. Emphasis on exercise, nutrition, stress management, and involvement. Intended for health teaching with older adults, but is useful for students in introductory courses who are studying concepts of health and wellness throughout the life span.

PRI Healthcare Education. Spectrum Films, Inc. P.O. Box 801, 2755 Jerrerson Street, Suite 103, Carlsbad, CA 92008. (619) 434-6191.

Student Attitudes in Working with Older Adults
Video $25
Developed for faculty to better appreciate students' attitudes about older
    adults. Reflects changes in student attitudes while working with older
    adults in community-based housing facilities. May also be used with
    Resident Council members to share student responses to learning
    about caring for older adults.
Instructional TV/Media Services, Lorain County Community College.
    1005 North Abbe Road, Elyria, OH. 44035

Time to Care
U-Matic & VHS 18 minutes $175 (1991)
Award-winning video which chronicles the educational growth of fourth-
    semester nursing students during a nursing home clinical experience.
    Captures students, clinical experiences as they work with residents.
    Useful to orient faculty and nursing home staff to placement of stu-
    dents in the nursing home, also excellent preparation for students
    prior to affiliation with a nursing home.
National League for Nursing. 350 Hudson St. New York NY. 10014.
    (800) 669-1656

Walk Me to the Water
VHS Black&White 30 minutes (1981)
Poignant portrayal of the unique experiences of three terminally ill can-
    cer patients being cared for at home. Patients and families tell their
    own stories. Show in small groups where tissues are available and
    there is time for a safe discussion.
Walk Me To The Water. P.O. Box 258, New Lebanon, NY 12125

What Do You See, Nurse?
VHS Color 12 minutes.
Based on the poem of the same name, it presents students and caregivers
    alike with a look at life in the nursing home as experienced by an
    elderly woman who pleads, "Look closer, see ME." Useful in the study
    of creating a therapeutic environment.
Coronety Film and Video. 420 Academy Drive, Northbrook IL 60062.

Current Films Available Through Local Video Stores

Nursing faculty report using movies now available on video that have issues related to aging as a theme or central to the plot.

Age-Old Friends. Vincent Gardenia and Hume Cronyn co-star in this film about two retirement home tenants whose bond of friendship unites them in their daily struggle with advancing years. Vignettes can be used in separate segments. (88 minutes).

Awakenings. Robin Williams and Robert DeNiro in a more or less true story of residents in a mental institution suffering from a form of encephalopathy who emerge from a trance after receiving L-Dopa. Powerful film which sparks a discussion about quality of life issues and the role of medical care in long-term, chronic illness. (Approx. two hours).

Dad. The relationship between an elderly father and his adult son intensifies when the father becomes ill. Selected vignettes (i.e., the ICU scene, the funeral) useful to illustrate choices about medical care and the resolution of family conflicts. (99 minutes).

Driving Miss Daisy. Story of a long-term relationship between an older southern widow and her chauffeur. Stars Jessica Tandy and Morgan Freeman. Deals with issues of prejudice and losses in aging. Sparks discussion about elements of a relationship. (115 minutes).

The Gin Game. Jessica Tandy is a resident of a rest home and develops a stormy friendship with another resident. Facilitates discussion about use of humor in relationships, communication patterns, and losses of aging. (Approximately 2 hours).

The Sunshine Boys. George Burns and Walter Mattheau review a friendship that is filled with anger, humor, and caring. Very touching final scene where they come to terms with their relationship. Helps students consider the strengths in a long term relationship that may not always be apparent. Very effective to just show the last scene, which is 14 minutes long.

A Trip to Bountiful. An aging woman (Geraldine Page) yearns to return to her childhood home in Bountiful, Texas one more time. She lives in a cramped city apartment with her distracted son and unsympathetic daughter-in-law, with whom she feuds. She takes off for Bountiful, outwitting her pursuers—a touching, adventuresome journey. The story is a wonderful study of aging, loneliness, and the "ageless self" concept developed by Sharon Kaufman.

Games

Into Aging. By Susan Dempsey-Lyle and Therese Hoffman. A simulation game that allows participants to experience vicariously the daily struggles of the elderly. There are three tables representing different aspects of elderly living: independent, semi-dependent, and dependent. All learners progress through the tables experiencing many losses along the way—physical, emotional, psychological, and material.

Although the word "game" usually connotes fun, *Into Aging* is neither fun or funny. The game evokes many feelings and is and excellent stimulus for discussion. There are clear directions for the facilitator; props are needed such as poker chips and tokens to represent different professions.

Charles B. Slack Publishing Co. 6900 Grove Road, Thorofare, NJ 08086.

Taking a Chance on the Later Years. By Mary O'Brien and Justine Bykowski. This is a table card game designed to sensitize participants to the differing needs of older people and the unpredictability of life events that hamper or enhance ability to maintain a satisfactory later life. Post-game discussion is essential.

Institute of Gerontology. University of Michigan. 520 East Liberty Street. Ann Arbor MI 48109.

Chapter 5

Other Resources: People and Organizations

There are a number of good reasons to become familiar with the network of organizations and individuals providing services to older persons. Instruction can be enriched through the judicious use of guest speakers and panelists, field trips, and out-of-class assignments. Useful publications directed to aging clients and their caretakers are published by a number of special interest organizations. Students will be better prepared for their future roles in the practice of nursing if they know about the community of agencies and organizations serving the elderly, know how to get more information, and know how to tell patients about sources of help. Gail Cobe, Ohlone College, prepared the following summary about the Area Agencies on Aging, and developed a list of the Geriatric Education Centers with their funding status at the time our resource guide went to press. In some instances, local GECs have provided a great deal of help to nursing faculty. It's worth exploring.

Area Agencies on Aging

The area agencies on aging (AAA's) were established by the Congress in 1973 to help coordinate those services to elders which are not covered by Social Security and Medicare. These federally funded services may include senior centers, meals on wheels, transportation systems, telephone reassurance, home care workers, counselors, and perhaps most important, information and referral services. There are over 600 AAA's and each city and county in the United States has one servicing it. You can obtain the name, address and phone number for your local area agency by calling your State Department of Aging. Sometimes, the local area agency on aging is listed in the phone book. We recommend that you become familiar with how your agency works. They will be able to provide you and your students with a macro view of the community resources in your area.

The Geriatric Education Centers

The Geriatric Education Centers are a nationwide network which offers education and training opportunities for health educators and health professionals to enhance access and quality of care for elders. Special emphasis is given by the GECs to the preparation of existing and new faculty members from educational institutions such as Community Colleges. These centers act as clearing houses and they develop and disseminate curriculum, audio visual and other teaching materials. Participants include nurses, physicians, dentists, social workers, pharmacists, occupation and physical therapists, podiatrists, dietitians and other allied health faculty, practitioners and students.

Geriatric Education Centers are supported by the Bureau of Health Professions, the Department of Health and Human Services, and they obtain funds through a competitive grant process.

We recommend that you call your regional GEC, speak with the director and inform him/her of your interests. They may have or be able to obtain curriculum materials which will help you with that well defined nursing home experience and geriatric nursing course. At the very least, make sure you are on their mailing lists, as their educational offerings are usually outstanding.

Geriatric Education Centers
Budget Period: 10/01/92 - 09/30/93

Harvard GEC
Harvard Medical School
Boston, MA 02115
(617) 432-1463

Western New York GEC
State Univ. of NY at
Buffalo, NY 14214
(716) 829-3176

Virginia GEC
Virginia Commonwealth
University
Richmond, VA 23298
(804) 786-9060

Hunter/Mt. Sinai GEC
Hunter College
New York, NY 10010
(212) 481-5142

Delaware Valley
Mid-Atlantic GEC
Philadelphia, PA 19104
(215) 898-3174

Meharry Consortium GEC
Nashville, TN 37208
(615) 327-6947

New Jersey GEC
University of Medicine &
   Dentistry of New Jersey
Stratford, NJ 08084
(609) 346-7141

GEC of Pennsylvania
University of Pittsburgh
Pittsburgh, PA 15260
(412) 624-2311

Miami Area GEC
University of Miami
Miami, FL 33136
(305) 545-0949

Mississippi GEC
University of Mississippi
Medical Center
Jackson, MS 39216
(601) 984-6190

Illinois GEC
University of Illinois at
   Chicago
Chicago, IL 60612
(312) 996-6698

Western Reserve GEC
Cleveland, OH 44120
(216) 368-5433

South Texas GEC
University of Texas Health
   Science Center
San Antonio, TX 78284
(512) 567-3370

Colorado GEC
University of Colorado
Denver, CO 80262
(303) 270-8974

Stanford GEC
Stanford University
Stanford, CA 94305
(415) 723-4489

Ohio Valley Appalachia
Regional GEC
University of Kentucky
Lexington, KY 40536
(606) 233-5156

Indiana GEC
Indiana University School
   of Medicine
Indianapolis, IN 46202
(317) 274-4702

Wisconsin GEC
Marquette University
Milwaukee, Wi 53233
(414) 288-3712

Texas Consortium of GEC
Baylor College of
   Medicine
Houston, TX 77030
(713) 798-6470

California GEC
University of California
Los Angeles, CA 90024
(310) 825-8255

Northwest GEC
University of Washington
Seattle, WA 98195
(206) 685-7478

University of Alabama at
   Birmingham GEC
Birmingham, AL 35294
(205) 934-1094

Minnesota Area GEC
University of Minnesota
Minneapolis, MN 55455
(612) 624-3904

Oklahoma GEC
University of Oklahoma
Oklahoma City, OK 73117
(405) 271-8558

Missouri Gateway GEC
St. Louis University
St. Louis, MO 63104
(314) 577-8462

Nevada GEC
University of Nevada at
   Reno
Reno, NV 89557
(702) 784-1689

Oregon GEC
Oregon Health Sciences
   University
Portland, OR 97201
(503) 721-7821

Geriatric Education Centers—*Alumni*

(GEC's not currently funded by the Bureau of Health Professions)

Appalachian GEC
Bowman Gray School of
  Medicine
Winston-Salem, NC
  27157
(919) 716-4284

Creighton Regional GEC
Creighton University
  School of Medicine
Omaha, NE
(402) 551-3772

Dakota Plains GEC
University of N. Dakota
Grand Forks, ND 58203
(701) 777-3200

Duke University GEC
Durham, NC 27710
(919) 684-5149

Great Lakes GEC
Chicago College of
  Osteopathic Medicine
Chicago, IL 60615
(312) 947-2708

Louisiana GEC
Louisiana State University
New Orleans, LA 70112
(504) 568-5842

Pacific Islands GEC
University of Hawaii,
  Manoa
Honolulu, HI 96817
(808) 523-8461

University of Florida GEC
Gainesville, FL 32610
(904) 395-0651

GEC of Michigan
Michigan State University
East Lansing, MI 48824
(517) 353-7780

Intermountain West GEC
University of Utah
College of Nursing
Salt Lake City, UT 84112
(801) 581-4064

New Mexico GEC
University of New Mexico
Albuquerque, NM 87131
(505) 277-5134

San Diego GEC
University of CA, San
  Diego
(213) 342-2964

University of So. Florida
  GEC
Tampa, FL 33612
(813) 974-4355

GEC of Puerto Rico
University of Puerto Rico
San Juan, Puerto Rico
(809) 751-2478

Iowa GEC
University of Iowa
  Hospitals and Clinics
Iowa City, IA 52242
(319) 356-1027

Pacific GEC
University of So. California
Los Angeles, CA 90033
(213) 342-2964

University of Connecticut
  GEC
Farmington, CT 06030
(203) 679-3956

Other Books of Interest from NLN Press

You may order NLN books by • TELEPHONE 800-NOW-9NLN, ext. 138
• FAX 212-989-3710 • MAIL Simply use the order form below

Book Title	Pub. No.	Price	NLN Member Price
☐ Teaching Gerontology: The Curriculum Imperative *Edited by Verle Waters*	15-2411	28.95	25.95
☐ Gerontological Nursing: Issues and Opportunities for the 21st Century *Edited by Mary M. Burke and Susan Sherman*	14-2510	27.95	24.95
☐ Determining the Future of Gerontological Nursing Education: Partnerships Between Education and Practice *Edited by Christine Heine*	14-2508	26.95	23.95
☐ Gerontology in the Nursing Curriculum *From the Community College/Nursing Home Partnership*	14-2506	6.95	5.95
☐ Mechanisms of Quality in Long-Term Care: Education *Edited by Ethel L. Mitty*	14-2550	25.95	22.95
☐ Quality Imperatives in Long-Term Care: The Elusive Agenda *Edited by Ethel L. Mitty*	41-2440	25.95	22.95
☐ Mechanisms of Quality in Long-Term Care: Service and Clinical Outcomes	41-2382	10.50	10.50
☐ Indices of Quality in Long-Term Care: Research & Practice	20-2292	20.95	18.95

PHOTOCOPY THIS FORM TO ORDER BY MAIL OR FAX

Photocopy this coupon and send with 1) a check payable to NLN, 2) credit card information, or 3) a purchase order number to: **NLN Publications Order Unit, 350 Hudson Street, New York, NY 10014 (FAX: 212-989-3710).**

Shipping & Handling Schedule	
Order Amount	**Charges**
Up to $24.99	$3.75
25.00-49.99	5.25
50.00-74.99	6.50
75.00-99.99	7.75
100.00 and up	10.00

Subtotal: $ ....

Shipping & Handling (see chart): $ ....

Total: $ ....

☐ Check enclosed ☐ P.O. #_____   ☐ NLN Member # (if appl.):_____

Charge the above total to ☐ Visa ☐ MasterCard ☐ American Express

Acct. #: _____ Exp. Date: _____

Authorized Signature: _____

Name _____ Title _____

Institution _____

Address _____

City, State, Zip_____

Daytime Telephone (_____) _____ Ext. _____